The Bull Within

A STORY OF BROTHERHOOD, GROWING UP,
AND RUNNING.

By: Devon Kelly

Order this book online at www.trafford.com
or email orders@trafford.com

Most Trafford titles are also available at major online book retailers.

Printed in the United States of America.

ISBN: 978-1-4269-6543-2 (sc)
ISBN: 978-1-4269-6544-9 (e)

Trafford rev. 06/14/2011

 www.trafford.com

North America & international
toll-free: 1 888 232 4444 (USA & Canada)
phone: 250 383 6864 ♦ fax: 812 355 4082

For my brothers that dared to believe

"Live your dreams; if anyone tries to tell you that you can't, screw 'em!" – Joe Newton

To the Thinclads of the Fall

By: Coach Kevin Keogh

I tip my hat to the thinly clad competitors, who battle others without special equipment, elaborate plays, regulated fields of play and other things which the sports fan have become so accustomed to seeing. These athletes battle opponents without the roar of the crowd to spur them on. They compete on uneven terrain in all kinds of weather--weather which would cancel other sports. Thinclads battle opponents constantly without having a time out or water break.

After learning these elements of the competition, one might ask, "What keeps them going". My reply would be: heart, teammates, and a love of one true sport which matches one competitor against another without having outside influences play a part in the final result.

A thinclad must have the heart of a true athlete who competes in the sport 365 days a year and does not gear up for a short season. These athletes run all year to achieve the success they desire. It is not a sometimes thing which one contemplates when one feels like it. This athlete must go out every day, sometimes twice a day, to become the athlete which they want to be. Sometimes this training is done alone and at varying times of the day. It takes heart to lace up those shoes and tackle what may seem at the time as a very unrewarding activity.

Another very important factor which keeps a thinclad going is the team which is represented. There is pride in representing your local community, school, parents, and others that one competes with. Unlike other sports, these thinclads do not play different positions, practice different drills, or work out at different locations. These thinclads are athletes who workout side by side doing the same work as their teammates. No one is special or different. Each does as much as they can together. Each one relies on the other to help get them through the work for the day. In this sport, the encouragement of teammates is essential to keeping one's spirit going in the light of difficult workout days. Teammates are not just people that one spends the season with and then has no contact with for the rest of the year. Thinclads are bound together tightly by the nature of the sport, the way they have to live to be able to compete in this sport, and by the respect each athlete gets from their teammates for their effort and commitment to the sport and this way of life.

A final concept which keeps a thinclad going has to be their love of the sport. This sport has been around for thousands of years. This sport is nothing new to mankind or an idea that was conjured up or developed to keep people busy or to get them involved in an activity. The thinclad loves to be in this sport which allows one to be outside in all seasons and battle with all the elements that nature has to offer. This sport does not have a coach choosing the starting line up or deciding who will play. All thinclads step to the line to compete at the same time. No athlete is granted a unique position or given any advantage over another athlete. How one did previously or marks achieved in the past only state what one is capable of doing. It is not always the best athlete who wins, but the one who is most prepared on that day—mentally and physically. In this true sport which matches one against another, an athlete cannot hide behind a winning score or hope that the effort of another teammate will influence the final result. In this sport, who one beats head to head, along with the time one achieves, determines a victory. This sport, unlike any other, allows each competitor to challenge and measure oneself every time they compete. It is also a sport where one is measured at the moment and not evaluated on previous or future projections of what might be.

Who are these thinclads who love the sport, rely on teammates, and have the heart to keep on going all year through all kinds of weather and other conditions which affect their lives? These thinclads of the fall are high school Cross Country runners seen many times by all of us as we go through our lives in our communities. These are boys and girls of the local community who run for the purest of reasons without the crowds to cheer them on as they workout and compete. These high school cross country runners are athletes who develop long lasting bonds of friendship with teammates. Through the years these bonds make them special friends forever and allow them to relive those special times when they were legends of the fall.

How do I know about this? For over 30 years I have been involved in high school cross country as a competitor and as a coach. I have those special cross country moments from the past which give me great pleasure and satisfaction in knowing that I was able to enjoy being a part of this great sport. As I look back at my life, many things could have been changed or could have been done without—but not high school cross country. It is a part of me which I will carry with me and cherish forever. So as I go along in my life, I tip my hat to the thinclads of the fall when I see them running down the sidewalks, in the streets, or through the parks of my town.

This Could be Something Special

One could sense change was in the air on an especially warm and balmy afternoon as spring near its end in Downers Grove, Illinois. The flowers and trees were in full bloom as the long hard winter finally lost its grip. The weather had taken its final turn to stay warm throughout the upcoming summer. Excitement pervaded through Downers Grove South High School in anticipation of the end of school and the upcoming summer. There was a sense that better things lay just around the corner. It was on this day that seven young men gathered out on the track at Downers Grove South. They met with a general feeling of eagerness, yet at the same time anxiety, as they all contemplated the task before them. Before they embarked on this great journey, first thing was first: they had to show their coach what they were made of, right here and now.

Coach Kevin Keogh wanted his top seven runners to run a two mile time trial. The long track season had just concluded and an even longer cross country season was only a couple weeks away from beginning. Coach Keogh wanted to see what he had on his hands going into summer training. Seven showed up but only six were running. Sophomore Devon Kelly had been running two mile races since January so he and Coach Keogh agreed before the race that they both knew where his ability was.

Juniors Ben Bouwman, his twin brother Nick, Jeff Vjevoda, Jon Hook, Joey Bicicchi, and sophomore Dave Kappel warmed up on the track together. Most of these six runners had been on varsity since they first joined the team at Downers Grove South High School. It had been their responsibility to score points and compete at the head of races since before they were even ready to do so. They knew that this upcoming season would be different. The five juniors only had one season left to live up to the hype that had accompanied them their freshman year. The last two cross country seasons had proved very disappointing. Injuries plagued the team. The top seven runners assembled on the track today had never even run a race together, but today they were ready for the simple task at hand. They all took the line, tense and quiet, in the waning moments before the race commenced.

Bang!

Coach Keogh fired the gun to start the race, and they were off. Usually a simple time trial was nothing to be excited about, but this one had some rather large implications. This would provide a glimpse at what had the potential to be the best cross country team ever at Downers Grove South. If only they knew how good they would be. If someone had told them what lay ahead, they wouldn't have believed it. No one would have believed it. But that would not come for many months. Right now, eight laps around the track would be the first step in their journey.

Jeff was very competitive, and he believed he could be the best runner on this team if he worked hard enough. He had started his high school career as a tall, lanky, uncoordinated freshman and worked his way up to be one of the best runners on the team. His competitiveness greatly aided and handicapped him. He challenged himself to run with the best runners in every race. Sometimes he could but sometimes he would sputter out half way through the race. Today, he felt determined to go out and be the best runner on the team going into the summer.

Unfortunately for him, Ben had been the best runner for two years now. Rarely did it occur that anyone on this team would beat him. As he stretched out his long legs and smoothly cruised around the track, he exuded confidence. He knew he was the best and never was afraid to let anyone know it. Today had a different outcome in store for Ben though. The two ran step for step with each other, both stubbornly refusing to slacken the pace. As the race unfolded, they began to separate away from the pack.

Joe came up next in third place. Joe drove himself with an intense desire to succeed. No amount of pain or misfortune could ever discourage him. His teammates respected the roaring fire that burnt in Joe's heart. His passion to succeed and help his teammates made him a natural leader and through his efforts, he established himself as a leader on the team. Today he was not feeling on top of his game for this race. He had been plagued by one injury after another since his freshman year, and he felt fatigued from trying to keep himself healthy for an entire season. As the heat resonated off the track Joe could feel his muscles tighten up as his pace slowed.

Not far behind Joe, Nick, Jon, and Dave had some troubles of their own. Jon had been captain and one of the best runners on the team since his sophomore season of cross country. He looked forward to once again enjoying a leading role on the team this upcoming season. His focus was not always consistent but when he put his mind to it, he could be a dominant runner.

Nick always ran with the burden of being in his twin brother's shadow. Ben would always be the standard people measured him up to. Regardless, Nick had made varsity for the first time the previous fall and dreamt of finally getting a chance to beat Ben in the fall. What Nick may have lacked in natural ability he made up for in mental strength. He could always be depended on to be toughing out a workout or running extra miles.

Dave had treaded a rough road to get to this point. After playing soccer in the fall of his freshman year, he went out for track and made varsity in the first race. After running varsity throughout his freshman track season, he injured himself over the summer and ran only two races in cross country. His track times from the spring had been slower than his times from his freshman year. Although somewhat discouraged, he knew if he could just stay healthy that he could be one of the best runners on the team.

As Devon watched from the infield he couldn't help but feel very intimidated and, at his very core, afraid of what he was watching. These guys were pretty fast and had been running competitively on this team since they had come in as freshman. Devon had not been fast at all his freshman year. He managed to make varsity his sophomore year through a lot of hard work and determination, but he still did not truly believe in himself. He knew he had to do something more to put himself in a place to compete and be successful. Dave had presented that opportunity for him. Dave convinced Devon to come with him to train with the team that had won twenty-four state titles, York High School. Their legendary coach invited runners throughout the state to come and experience the training York did every summer that rivaled the training programs of many colleges. Devon still had trouble believing he could keep up with most of his own teammates: how was he going to make it through this York Camp?

The time trial came down to the final lap. Ben and Jeff had been running away from everyone else for most of the race. They came in dead even. Jeff felt elated. He could not believe he had just run stride for stride with the team's fastest runner. As the others came in they did not find their races so impressive. Joe, Jon, Nick, and Dave felt worn down from the countless miles they had put in over the track season. This race was not their best.

As the runners griped about their performances, Coach Keogh quietly thought to himself. After twenty-seven years of coaching, Kevin Keogh had seen plenty of good teams, and he was looking at one right now. All six of them had finished within one minute of each other.

That was incredible.

A cross country team's points are scored by the places of its top five runners. What place they get equals how many points they score (First place = 1 point; Second place = 2 points, etc.). The team that has the lowest score is the team that has the lowest place numbers. Coach Keogh was looking at seven runners who could all finish within a minute of each other and record some great scores in the fall. He knew even though Devon didn't run that he had run times week in and week out over the track season that would have put him right in the mix with the other six today. Coach Keogh was looking at a team that could win conference, and possibly for only the second time in his long coaching career, go to State.

Champions are made in the Summer

Dave Kappel and Devon Kelly made a controversial decision by going to York Camp. They risked losing the respect of their teammates by not training with them; they risked hurting themselves by undergoing training far more difficult than anything they had ever done before; they didn't even really know what they were getting into. They had known about this training program before but always just disregarded it as something that other people did. It either wasn't for them or they would never make it through. They couldn't even imagine the kind of insane training that had produced just short of half of the last fifty Illinois state cross country champions. That all changed because of one man.

Dr. Mike Calcagno was a chiropractor and physical therapist. He was well known for treating athletes' injuries and getting them back on the field as quickly as possible. Because of this well deserved reputation he was the York cross country teams's unofficial team doctor. The best team in the state wanted the best treatment possible. He was also known for being a very inspirational man. Mike Calcagno had been an All-American linebacker while at the same time working his way through college to pay his tuition. He built one of the best physical therapy centers in Illinois from the ground up with his brother. He filled in sometimes for York's head coach and did a masterful job of doing so. From being such a successful person and treating some of the best athletes in the state, he knew how to recognize special people when he came across them. Dr. Calcagno saw two of these special people come into his office in the spring of that year.

Dave and Devon had both been riddled with injuries since they began running. Dave had been slowed by a nagging hamstring injury that he could not get rid of. The injury cost him almost the entire cross country season from the previous fall and considerably slowed his times in track. Devon had pulled or sprained almost every possible muscle that was involved with running. If he was getting over one injury then another one would spring up. He missed a month of the indoor track season because of a foot problem that no doctor could figure out. Dave and Devon were both sick of these ongoing health problems. They knew how successful they could be if they could only stay healthy.

Word got to Dave's parents about this Dr. Calcagno. All of the other physical therapists Dave had seen could not seem to help him heal. Dr. Calcagno had a very good reputation amongst the state's top runners so Dave decided to give him a shot. After just a few months of seeing the good Dr. Calcagno, or Dr. Mike as he liked to be called, Dave could not believe the results. He referred Devon to Dr. Mike, and he saw the same results.

Another gift Dr. Mike possessed was the ability to persuade people. He recognized the potential in both Dave and Devon and wanted to see them succeed. Dr. Mike knew the results that York Camp could produce and knew that Devon and Dave would be up to the task if they put their minds to it. Dr. Mike convinced Dave to go, but Dave did not want to do this alone. He wanted his friend and running partner to be there with him. Dr. Mike approached Devon about going to York Camp one day during his physical therapy session and, after a very short debate, Devon agreed to go.

Devon and Dave arrived at their first day of York Camp not long after the two mile time trial. They made the forty minute drive north with their friend Jake. Jake was a collegiate runner and looking to get an edge on his competition as well. The three of them walked up and checked in with Coach Joe Newton. Coach Joe Newton was someone that a person could never forget after meeting him just once. At the age of seventy-eight he had more intensity and passion for life than most people ever will. This would be his fiftieth year of coaching, and his resume was quite impressive. Along with his twenty-four state titles he had been the only high school coach to ever be on an Olympic coaching staff; which he had done at the Soeul, Korea Olympics in 1988. He had been trusted to take care of and train Olympian runner Sebastian Coe who won gold at the 1984 Los Angeles Olympic Games. He had sent dozens of runners to college, produced more All-State runners, conference trophies, as well as second and third place finishes at State than all of the rest of the coaches in Illinois combined.

Mr. Newton, as he insisted his runners call him, enthusiastically greeted Dave and Devon. He told them to sit down, and they anxiously waited for practice to start. Everyday Mr. Newton gave a thought for the day, and the first one Dave and Devon ever heard was one they would never forget. "Everyday a man chooses to be mediocre, good, or great. If you choose to be mediocre then that's all you're ever going to be!" These words seared into the two friends' minds and were to keep them motivated through pain and exhaustion they could not even begin to comprehend.

They sat among at least two hundred other runners from across the state. Almost one hundred-fifty of which were from York's team alone! Mr. Newton gave the workout for the day. They were to run for forty-five minutes, take a five minute break, run for another forty-five minutes, take another five minute break, and then do a cool down run for thirty minutes at the end.

What? Devon and Dave were not sure they heard the old coach correctly. Was he serious? At Downers South practices, forty-five minutes was a run, not the first segment of one. This sounded insane. How were they going to make it through this?

They started off the run completely unsure of what to expect from this. They were not even in very good shape. They ran a total of three days the previous week after taking off two weeks after the time trial. The laps started rolling by as Dave and Devon settled in. They were not going to worry themselves about anything but this first segment. The run started to drag on until they heard the whistle to signal the end of the segment. This was just the end of the first segment. They got some water and, before they knew it, the time had come to start the next segment. Surprisingly, this one seemed to get easier as it went on. They both began to feel somewhat comfortable and were able to run this segment until the end as well. The cool down was no problem after that.

They finished this run having put in almost sixteen miles. That was usually the mileage the two of them would run in two days. To top that off, they ran four miles in the afternoon. Two-a-day runs were another part of York's summer training regimen. Their minds were made up. Never had they been so determined. They knew in their hearts that they were going to make it through this York Camp. They were going to run alongside champions and be coached by legends.

They ended the week having run almost ninety miles. That was double their maximum mileage for any single week ever. Their bodies knew a new definition of weariness. Their minds had a new definition of toughness. Their hearts had a new definition of desire. That was only the first week.

Practice Starts at Downers South

While Dave and Devon went to their first day of York Camp, the rest of the Downers South Mustangs' varsity runners met at school for their first practice of the summer. The five other seniors that made up the rest of the varsity team had been together for three years now. They had been part of a tremendous freshman class, better than any the school had ever seen. A lot of excitement originally followed these freshman phenoms, but they had yet to live up to the hype they created for themselves. A weak group of upperclassman their sophomore year called for them to be moved up to varsity before they were ready. Joe dislocated his hip, Jeff was hampered by sickness, and many of them were not ready to handle to responsibility that being a varsity runner demanded. Their junior year Joe hurt himself again. Dave, that year's new addition, got hurt during his first year of doing cross country so the team was incomplete once again. This year was it. All the pieces were in place. They all had the talent. They just needed to stay healthy and work hard.

Joe, still troubled by injury problems, chose to run at O'brien Park, the team's home course located in a park down the street from the high school. He did this because running on the grass felt much easier on his fragile shins that were recovering from stress fractures that had held him out of last year's season. Out of all the seniors, Joe knew Dave and Devon the best, and he understood why they were running at York Camp instead of with the team. He could not lie to himself that he desired to join them.

Joe had always been a hard worker. He was the youngest in a family that prided itself on hard work and the results that come with it. Joe was known as being one of the toughest and hardest working runners in state. This stubborn work ethic had brought about his injuries in the past. His refusal to give up no matter what helped and hindered him throughout his career.

His daily runs at O'brien Park were long and gave him plenty of time to think. He knew he could be working harder and running with Dave and Devon at York. Joe felt torn between his loyalty to his team as one of the captains and his determination to train as hard as he possibly could. In the early weeks of the summer, this dilemma played out in Joe's head daily.

The rest of the team felt content with doing the training they had always been doing. It had helped them improve and become successful already, and they didn't see why they should change. There was a bit of resentment towards Dave and Devon. The two of them were looked at as trying to defy what the rest of the team was doing. The rest of the team didn't understand why they weren't training with their teammates. How could they build a great team when all of them weren't even running together?

As the early weeks of the summer passed, the seniors began to grow apart. Joe would go off and do his own runs on grass at O'brien Park. Sometimes Jeff or Jon would join him but, more times than not, Joe ran on his own. Jon worked in a pharmaceutical internship at the insistence of his father. Splitting time between the internship and running was not easy, and time after time he found himself sacrificing his daily run to get some extra sleep before going to work every morning. As a team captain, Jon knew he should be setting a better example, and it bothered him that he was not putting in the work he should be. A couple weeks into the summer Jeff left to go on a long vacation with his family. With Jeff gone on vacation and Jon showing up only a few days every week, the varsity runners that attended practice at Downers South dwindled down to three, and they were about to lose one more

The Will to Prepare

Meanwhile, Dave and Devon could not believe the lengths they pushed their bodies to at York Camp. It felt like they surpassed a new physical milestone every day. In just a few short weeks they went from thinking forty miles was a good total for the week to forty miles being their usual total after two days. They accumulated anywhere from eighty to one hundred miles per week. Their legs gained speed and strength they never believed they could have possessed. Most importantly, they started to believe that they could be champions.

This newfound confidence came from doing world class workouts with world class athletes. They heard motivational advice everyday for free that most people pay thousands of dollars to hear. Mr. Newton's thoughts for the day made them feel like they could achieve anything. Sayings such as: "Live your dreams; if anyone tries to say you can't then screw 'em!;" and, "The secret of success in life is for a man to be ready when his opportunity comes;" inspired determination and focus such as Dave and Devon had never felt. They believed they could achieve feats that they had only dreamed about.

The body of work they put in day in and day out was unbelievable. An average week would start off with running twenty-five quarter mile laps around the track almost as fast as they could go, with only one minute to rest in between. This workout made a man out of those who had the courage to last the whole way through. This was done in the hot summer sun on a track that would, on average, be at least ten degrees hotter than the actual temperature. They would recover the next day with a fast paced twelve to sixteen mile run. The next day was a ten mile speed workout. The next day consisted of long intervals of between 1200 meters and a mile on the track again. Friday was another twelve to sixteen mile run, and the week capped off with a hill workout on Saturday morning. All of this was done while running four miles in the afternoon everyday that they ran in the morning.

Their bodies constantly ached from the daily punishment they endured. Their legs felt so sore that it would be hard to get out of bed in the morning. Their backs ached from the pounding that one-hundred mile weeks put on them. Sometimes it felt as if every muscle in their body was sapped of its energy. Regardless, they pushed forward every day. Within a few short weeks they could not believe the results they were seeing. This kept their spirits high and gave them the will to carry on.

Dave and Devon would often run with Joe on their afternoon runs and tell him about everything they did at York Camp. They both respected Joe very much. Joe had helped convince Dave to start running and encouraged Devon when he saw how serious he was becoming. Dave and Devon wanted Joe to do York Camp with them. They knew how hard he worked, and they knew that he would love what they were doing at York. As the three of them grew closer, Joe felt more of a desire to follow his teammates up to this camp to see what they kept raving about.

Finally, Joe agreed to come with them one day. He never looked back. This was exactly what he had been looking for. Being at York Camp made one feel as if they were in the presence of excellence. The three friends felt as if by just being there, the greatness of all of those running legends that had come through York would just transfer onto them. It made one feel as if they were a part of the storied history of the program, and it was everything Joe had been longing for his whole high school career. He was hooked, and for the rest of the summer it would be these three making the drive up to York Camp with their friend Jake every day

The Tripod

Dave, Joe, and Devon immediately formed a close camaraderie which made all of the countless miles that they ran for the rest of the season feel just a little bit easier. They ran together, motivated each other, and hung out together after practice. One of them was seldom seen without the other two being close by. They all shared the same goal and had the same desire to achieve that goal. They wanted to go to State.

State was something that Joe's father, who was an all-state runner in high school, often spoke of. State was the promised land for a high school runner. It was the only time all year that the best runners in the state would all line up on the same starting line. It was where tears of the joy of victory and the shame of defeat were simultaneously shed. This was where Dave, Joe, and Devon dreamed of going. As they often joked, nothing could topple over the tripod.

With Joe now running at York with Dave and Devon, Joe's father began to take extra interest in the team. His father, Glenn, had been around running for many years and knew what champions looked like and what great teams were made out of. Glenn had been assistant coach during Joe's freshman and sophomore years but took the previous fall off in order to be with Joe and help him heal his fractured shins. This year Glenn wanted to be a part of the team again. He knew the talent was there, and there was no denying the desire to win amongst these seven runners. Glenn had known all of the seniors since they were freshman, and he was getting to know Dave and Devon very well also. These were special individuals that required extra attention. A great team requires great leadership, and Glenn could provide that.

Glenn possessed the gift of being a great motivational speaker. He had this gift from overcoming much adversity and difficulty in his running career. The Downers South teams that Glenn had been assistant coach with the previous two years did not understand his motivational speeches because they did not believe they were great. Their hearts were not dedicated to success. This team was different. Glenn knew that these seven individuals could be great if someone could help them realize just how much potential they had. Glenn spent the rest of the summer thinking of how he could help bring this team to State. Before this team could believe in the great things they were capable of, they needed to first of all believe in each other. That seemed like an insurmountable task after one Saturday in late June.

The Divisions Run Deep

The varsity runners that were still showing up at Downers South to practice were down to Ben and Nick Bouwman and sometimes Jon when he wasn't working. The three of them could see that the team was very much divided. Dave, Joe, and Devon had completely stopped showing up at all at Downers South. Jon and the Bouwmans agreed that something needed to be done to bring the team together. They had not all been together since the time trial they ran at the end of the track season. Jon called the varsity team members one Friday night and said that they all needed to run together at least once. He convinced them all to meet the next morning at a forest preserve that that they often ran at.

Grudgingly, Dave, Joe, and Devon deviated from their usual Saturday hill workout with York to meet with their team. Once everyone showed up there was instant conflict. They all had great pride in the work they had been putting in and were at odds with each other. Devon and Ben were bickering over who would be the faster runner in the upcoming season. Joe snapped at someone for making a remark about being too heavy from lifting weights. As the run started it seemed it would be a miracle if they made it through all ten miles without killing each other.

This run had the complete opposite effect Jon and the Bouwmans had hoped for. Something that made this team great was that all seven of them believed they could be the best. Today, this tore them apart. They were all angry at each other and Ben, Nick, and Jon instantly sped ahead of the other three. Devon went hard after them, stubbornly wanting to show Ben who was tougher and faster. As Joe and Dave ran at an easy pace in the rear they knew this was not good. The team looked like they would be fortunate to simply make it through the season in one piece much less come together and learn to trust each other. No words were spoken after the run was over, and they went their separate ways. This was a serious problem that needed to be addressed before they had any hopes of achieving greatness.

Easing the Tension

About a week and a half after the failed team bonding run, Dave, Joe, and Devon had the day off from York Camp because of the Fourth of July. The three of them met with the rest of the Downers South team at the school. There were no heated exchanges, but there were not any friendly apologies either. Devon, being very stubborn and proud, had no problems showing his disdain for Ben after their conflict a week and a half ago. The other members of the team could sense the tension that existed amongst them and when the run began they went separate ways. Jon ran with the three York Camp runners while the Bouwmans took off with the rest of the team. Jeff was still gone on vacation.

While on the run, Jon talked with Dave, Joe, and Devon about the training they had been doing. For the first time he had a real appreciation for the work they were putting in. He realized that they had not done this to rebel from the team. They truly wanted to help this team succeed and were doing everything they could to make that happen.

Jon decided to give another shot at bringing the team together. He invited them all over to a bar-be-que at his house. Finally, they came together on some common ground without being at each other's throats. Perhaps there was hope that they all could learn to respect each other. They needed to learn how to work with each other instead of against each other. It couldn't always be about competing over who is faster and who is working harder. A great team must learn to respect each other on and off of the field of competition. A team that is divided is a team that fails, and this team was too good to allow themselves to fail.

Two weeks later many members from the team attended a week-long running camp put on by the University of Wisconsin. All of the varsity members besides Ben attended this camp along with many other members of the team. This was something fun that was more about just getting away and having a good time together. This did more than anything to bring them all closer.

They managed to put aside their differences for the week. They would ditch mandatory lectures and group meetings to go swimming together, and stayed up late at night trying to sneak around after they were required to be in their rooms. Also, for the first time all summer, they ran together. Almost all of the varsity members got placed in the same skill level group and were able to just run together without letting their petty conflicts come between them. At the end of the week all of the team, varsity or not, felt the week away brought them closer together. As they arrived back at Downers Grove South reality set back in.

Bittersweet Homecoming

York Camp was over so Dave, Joe, and Devon returned to Downers Grove South to practice with their teammates. For the first two weeks before the season starts all Illinois high school sports coaches are not allowed to be with their teams so it would be up to the athletes to run things themselves. This proved to be problematic.

Devon, his ego swelled with an excessive amount of pride and arrogance, stepped up on the first day back at practice and boldly proclaimed that things would be different. He said that the team would now be doing the workouts that he, Dave, and Joe had done at York, and the old way of doings at Downers South was over. Not surprisingly, this did not go over well with everyone else, especially with an alumni runner who was there that day. He and Devon got into a heated exchange over what the right kind of training was and who knows best. These egos were too big to for either side to settle and the alumni runner stormed off, cursing back at Devon.

This argument had just polarized the varsity team once again. Some sided with the alumni and others sided with Devon. Now that they were all back at home, their differences had arisen once again. They had all come together at Wisconsin Camp, but now things were just going on the way they had been all summer. They were running together but did not have the amount of respect for each other they needed to have.

Kevin Keogh spoke with Glenn Bicicchi, the two having recently agreed that Glenn would be assistant coach, about their team. They both saw these differences coming between their runners and knew something needed to be done to fix this.

Alumni Meet

At the end of every summer Coach Keogh held an alumni race at O'brien Park. The alumni race was always held in mid-August on the last Friday before coaches were allowed to be with their teams again. The race pitted the Downers South alumni against the current runners on the team. It was a way for alumni to come back and pay homage to Coach Keogh as well as an opportunity to reunite old friends. This was also a way to gauge where the varsity team was at just before the official practices started.

The runners still had their differences with each other but were ready to race. Jeff finally returned but would not be running because he had not been putting in the kind of work he should have been while on vacation. The other six knew they were ready. They had all been working especially hard in the last few weeks and wanted to showcase their ability. This alumni meet had more energy surrounding it than was usually characteristic of this race. Traditionally, the alumni meet was a laid back race that was more fun than competitive, but this was not a traditional year. The coaches knew this team was special, and the time had finally come to see what they were made of after a long summer of training. The runners had been at each other's throats for most of the summer and were anxious to finally back up all of their big talk.

Dave, Joe, and Devon felt an extra amount of pressure. They had been the rebels of the team, foregoing practicing with the team to do York Camp. It was time to see how much they really had improved. Devon had boasted about how superior their training was to the rest of the team so it was time to back up all of his talk. Dave was about to start his first complete cross country season, and the expectations for him to perform were tremendous. Joe was down to his last year, and after two seasons that had been cut short by injury, he needed to make this season count. While doing their warm-ups all three of them felt a heavy weight on their shoulders.

Ben felt confident in his ability to succeed today. He fully expected to come out and lead this race from start to finish. Jon and Nick on the other hand were just as uneasy as the three York Camp runners. They felt threatened by the brashness and arrogance of some of the other runners on the team. Nick worried that his training had not been enough to keep up with the everyone else. He made some bold statements himself that he felt pressured to back up. Jon knew he had not put in the necessary work over the summer and just hoped he could keep up for most of the race. The six varsity runners took the line with the alumni and other members from the Downers South team. As Coach Keogh addressed the crowd, Ben, Nick, Jon, Joe, Dave, and Devon could not wait for him to fire the gun to start the race. Coach Keogh finished introducing all of the contestants and told them to step to the line.

Bang!

He wasted no time in firing the gun. The runners were off. Ben immediately took the lead with the alumni that had clashed with Devon two weeks earlier as the rest of the team fell into place. Devon, Dave, and Nick ran together and established a good pace. For the first mile or so they moved comfortably with each other. About ten meters behind, Joe kept pace with another alumni runner. He was nervous and trying to get comfortable before he started quickening his pace. Jon trailed behind Joe but still established a pretty strong pace. He was hoping he would surge forward soon enough and catch up.

The runners were about a mile and a half into the race. Ben had already put the race away. No one would catch him. Dave and Devon were trying to pull ahead of Nick. Nick had claimed that he would beat them just a few days earlier, and they were anxious to make him eat his words. They saw a hill coming up and knew this was their opportunity to make a move. Their training over the summer had undoubtedly made them much stronger. They had done hill workouts every Saturday for two months so this was nothing for them. They approached the base of the hill and hit it hard. They put their heads down, pushed off their toes, and left Nick behind. As they descended down the other side of the hill someone came up next to them. It was Joe. The three friends ran together once again. They ran the rest of the race together and crossed the finish line in unison. Nick finished about thirty seconds behind them. Jon was not far behind him. Ben finished in second place to the top alumni runner by just three seconds. The team had run their first race together and had done something no other team at Downers South had ever done.

As they watched the runners finish the race, Coaches Keogh and Bicicchi could not help but notice many of their runners were finishing ahead of the alumni. Usually, the alumni meet was not even close between the alumni and high school runners. The collegiate runners would typically win by a considerable margin, but today was much closer than usual. The Downers South runners finished ahead of the alumni in many places. The tripod of Dave, Joe, and Devon had helped score considerable points for Downers South. They had placed in fourth, fifth, and sixth place. The all important fifth runner for Downers South had not been far behind. The fifth runner is extremely important in scoring for cross country because the closer the fifth runner was to the first runner, the better the score would be.

Downers South's split was very good. In fact, it was better than the alumni. For the first time ever in the history of Downers Grove South cross country, the high school runners had beat the alumni. Coach Keogh and Coach Bicicchi looked at each other and both thought the same thing. This team was something special.

Purgatory Rocks at the Indiana Dunes

The 1983 Downers Grove South cross country team had been the best the school had ever fielded. They remained the only Downers South team to qualify for the State Meet. Something they did that had brought them close together was run at Indiana Dunes State Park in north-western Indiana, right on Lake Michigan. This had been a fun way for all of them to get in shape and just have a good time together. The members of the current team talked of doing this all summer and finally were able to arrange for this to happen the day after the alumni meet.

Ben and Nick Bouwman volunteered to have the team sleep over at their house Friday night after the alumni meet and drive them all to the dunes in their van the next morning. Everyone's spirits were high after their victory at the alumni meet, and they were all excited for a day of running and swimming in Lake Michigan. After an eventful night of keeping each other awake and playing pranks on the ones that actually fell asleep, the team piled into the Bouwman's mini-van and set out for the dunes.

Nick drove which proved problematic very soon into the trip. He did not have too many hours behind the wheel and was very nervous driving on the highway. Ben was in charge of directions which was not his area of expertise either. After driving for about half an hour Ben told Nick to turn off of the highway. He took the exit and after getting off of the highway the team quickly realized this was not anything close to the Indiana Dunes.

They had turned off into an urban neighborhood somewhere in Indiana. They were nowhere near the Indiana Dunes. To make things even better, there was construction on all of the entrances going back to the highway so they drove around in circles trying to find a way to get back on the highway. It took almost an hour and a half until Nick finally found a way to get back onto the highway. Everyone was tired of sitting in the back of this van. If they had actually stayed on the highway and gone the right way they would be at the dunes by now. Some wanted to head back but the consensus was to carry on towards their destination.

The team finally arrived at the dunes but these were not the dunes most of them had envisioned. These dunes, which the Bouwmans had been going to for years, were nicely

20

sandwiched between a nuclear power plant and some kind of factory. Indiana Dunes State Park, where most of them thought they were going, was huge. The beachfront offered plenty of space to run on as well as several large dunes. This place was not that. The beachfront was not very long and one could run across the entire park in ten minutes. There was grumbling amongst some of the team members that were expecting a picturesque state park. This trip had already been very interesting, and they had just arrived at the place they were supposed to be almost two hours ago.

They managed to do their run and spent the rest of the day messing around and trying to forget they were swimming in water that was most likely polluted with chemicals. They played ultimate fris-bee, swam in the lake, and buried Dave in the sand. Dave cracked everyone up after digging up a rock in the sand and exclaiming that he had dug to purgatory to find it. The mood was light for the rest of the day. It wasn't about running, competing against each other, or going to State. Today they were just a group of friends hanging out at the beach and having a good time. This was the first time all seven varsity runners had been together and just enjoyed themselves. Judging by the relations between them for most of the summer, this was nothing short of a miracle. Finally, they were starting to come together.

Official Practice Begins

The team had been meeting throughout the summer and Coach Keogh attended many of those practices, but the coaches were not allowed to hold mandatory practices until two weeks before school started. The whole team assembled at Downers Grove South for their first official practice together. Coach Keogh and Coach Bicicchi addressed the team and made one thing clear; this season was going to be different.

Coach Keogh and Bicicchi met a couple days earlier to discuss the upcoming season. They both agreed that this team was unlike any other Coach Keogh had ever coached in his twenty-nine years of experience. Coach Bicicchi insisted that they could be pushed harder than any team had been pushed at Downers South. Coach Keogh agreed to this and both of them completely agreed on one thing: the goal was to make it to State. With a group this talented nothing less should be expected. As they drew up the workout schedule they knew that they would push their runners to the brink. The two expected goals from putting them through such physical anguish were to get them in world-class shape by the end of the season and bring them together by running all of the resentment out of them.

The team assembled in anticipation of their first practice. The workout for the day would be mile repeats. Every mile repeat they ran was agonizing. Dave, Joe, and Devon had been worried that the practices back at Downers South would be too easy for them after practicing with York all summer; their worries were put to rest after this practice. After the first two repeats, it was obvious who was in the best shape. Jeff had been on vacation all summer and was far behind the rest of the varsity team. Ben was leading but Joe, whose best track event was the mile, was not far behind. Nick, Dave, Devon, and Jon jostled for position behind Ben and Joe. Even though Jon was not in as good of shape as the other three that he was running with, he kept up. This was a grueling workout. Coach Bicicchi had to keep them motivated in between intervals to keep them going. After three repeats, Coach Keogh looked over at Coach Bicicchi and said, "enough?" Coach Bicicchi simply replied, "more."

More was what they received. After finishing his last mile, Joe collapsed from exhaustion. The rest of the team was not in much better shape. After four mile repeats Joe and Ben averaged between 4:55 and 5:00 minutes for every mile. Nick, Dave, Devon, and Jon were averaging between 5:10 and 5:15. The surprise of the day was sophomore Steve Schmid who would be running cross country for the first time. He kept pace with Jeff on almost every mile.

Coach Keogh and Coach Bicicchi addressed the varsity after practice. They laid down the ground rules for the season. They made it clear that these seven runners were going to be the group that would be expected to do great things. If this team was going to State, it was going to be with these seven young men leading the way. Coach Keogh made it clear that they were to live and breathe cross country for the next two and a half months. Cross country was to become their life. Their family was the team, and their home was the home course at O'Brien Park. Coach Bicicchi made one last thing clear. They were to stay away from girls. This team could not afford distractions or someone getting sick and missing time. The season rested with these seven athletes and together they would stand or fall. They were going to have to sacrifice much if they really wanted to achieve the goals they spoke of reaching. The order to stay away from girls was a bitter pill for most of them to swallow. They were learning to like each other but…not that much. It was going to be a long season.

A few days later Coach Keogh was gone to take care of his grandchildren, and Coach Bicicchi had health problems that he was seeking treatment for that day, so it was just the team and Assistant Coach Billy Hois. There was already some dissension at the start of practice. Since Coach Keogh and Bicicchi were gone some members of the varsity hoped to cut the planned workout of twelve half-mile intervals short. Some other members of the team did not see eye-to-eye with this mentality. Outspoken Devon made his feelings clear on the situation. He did not want anyone giving a subpar performance out here today. His heart was set on going to State and no one was going to interfere with this goal as long as he had something to say about it.

Devon's remarks were not well received by Ben. Ben did not like how much work they were doing, did not like doing it at O'Brien Park, and most of all, did not like other people telling him what to do. He determined that he would show the rest of the team how much this workout meant to him. The plan was to do six half-miles in one direction and do the last six in the opposite direction so they would not put too much strain one side of their bodies. After making an effort to lead the first six by as much distance as possible, Ben did not go in the opposite direction with the rest of the team. He wanted to make a statement that he did not need to do this new workout plan. He believed what he was used to doing was fine, and he wanted to keep doing that.

Ben's choice to go against the team did not sit well with many of his teammates. After the workout many members of the varsity had much to say about Ben's act of protest. Some were even bold enough to degrade Ben in front of his brother who did not appreciate that whatsoever. The team left practice that day divided once again. Would these egos ever be able to put aside their differences? It had been three months, and it seemed that any progress that had been made was negated by this practice. The team headed home. The first meet of the season was coming up and the 2005 Downers Grove South Mustangs cross country team had a long way to go before they could call themselves a team.

The Team Unveils Itself

The team had continued to look good in workouts, but the unity still remained a work in progress. The coaches even had disputes amongst themselves. The circumstances for the team were less than ideal approaching the Lyons Township Invite. Along with the personal rivalries that still existed between the team members, some of them were not in ideal mental and physical health. Joe had infected his toenail at the dunes two weeks before and had to get it surgically removed. The doctors suggested he take a couple weeks off to let it heal. Joe ran later that day. Running caused almost excruciating pain for Joe's toe. The skin that his removed toenail had covered was completely raw and anything rubbing against caused a great deal of pain. Despite this, he continued to practice and lead workouts every day.

Many of the runners did not feel very confident before the race. Jeff was worried that his lack of preparation over the summer might cost him his spot on varsity. Steve Schmid had been consistently nipping at his heels in practice and wanted his spot on varsity. Despite all of the work they had put in Devon and Dave were still nervous. Devon still had trouble believing that he was really a good runner. On top of his lack of confidence, Devon's thoughts drifted to his family in New Orleans. Hurricane Katrina had just hit New Orleans, and Devon had many family members that lived there. He had yet to hear from them. Jon might have been in the worst shape mentally out of all of them. For no apparent reason he felt terrified before the Lyons Township race and could not figure out why.

The team woke up on race day unsure of what to expect. They boarded the bus at 7:30 a.m. and set out with much uncertainty surrounding them. The varsity race was the last race of the day so the top seven had to wait for almost four hours before their chance finally came. During pre-race warm-ups their thoughts drifted to their various concerns. Today was their shot to come out and show the state that they were a team to be reckoned with. The preseason team rankings had been released and the Downers Grove South Mustangs were not anywhere to be seen in the top 25. There were no expectations from any other schools for Downers South. Their teams for the last few seasons had been nothing worth speaking of. Ben had individually qualified for State the year before, and that was all anyone knew of the team.

The team lined up in their starting box, did their practice starts, and listened to their pre-race pep talk from Coach Keogh and Bicicchi. The message from the coaches was clear; today is your shot to prove what you're made of, so get it done.

Bang!

The starter fired the gun and the race was off. Early on, the team from Carl Sandburg High School was clearly ahead. Ben was the only one from the Downers South team in the top ten. Dave and Joe fought to get into the top ten. Devon, Nick, and Jeff ran together around twentieth place, and Jon was nowhere to be seen. Jon had felt tense and apprehensive the entire four hours before the race, and his feelings only worsened throughout the course of the race. Jon, normally a very aggressive runner, ran very timidly. He felt overwhelmed by the expectations surrounding this team. He feared that he would not be good enough to compete with the other six members of the varsity team. These bad thoughts swirled in his head as one racer after another passed him by.

Joe's toe hurt intensely, but he still pushed through the pain. Just as he began to believe he could tough out this race, another team's runner accidentally stepped on his bad toe with their running spikes. The pain was awful. His toe bled so profusely that his shoe was soaked in blood. This was just too painful, even for Joe. He began to fall back in the race. Much to Jeff's surprise he kept pace with Nick and Devon. He was a very strong runner, and his strength and determination carried him through this race. Nick and Devon felt comfortable and started to pull away. Devon believed in himself more and more with every step. It came down to about half a mile to go. Ben cruised to a third place finish, Dave pushed hard and crossed the line in twelfth place, and Devon pulled away from the middle pack. He had run ahead of Nick and was chasing down another team's runner. Devon had always been at his best at the end of races. No matter what, his finishing kick was always something to watch out for. The runner next to Devon was in pain, and Devon knew it. His breathing was labored and his feet were stomping on the ground as if he had weights in his shoes. It was time for Devon to move. With two hundred meters to go Devon began to sprint. He narrowly pulled ahead of a runner from Carl Sandburg High School to finish in fifteenth place. Nick and Jeff crossed the line just a few seconds behind him. Joe labored to a respectable finish, and Jon finished much further back.

Downers South finished with their top five in the top twenty places. They earned second place at the meet. This turned some heads from Carl Sandburg's team. They had run at state the year before and wanted to know who this upstart team was that just gave them a run for their money. Ben looked like he was going to be all-state. Dave, Nick, and Devon knocked more than a minute off of their best times from the year before. Jeff finished fifth on the team while improving more than thirty seconds from his best time the year before. Joe managed to run a good race considering his toe was in extreme pain and bleeding profusely the entire race. Jon on the other hand did not fare so well. He barely beat his best time from the previous year.

The next night Jon, still upset from his race, had some of the guys from the team over at his house for a bon fire. Jon wanted to take his anger out on something. He was a team captain and was one of the best runners on the team from the year before. He knew he was in shape and should not have run like he had the day before at Lyons Township. He felt determined to take out his frustration with some kind of destructive act. While everyone was at his house, he went out to the garage and filled a water bottle with gasoline. He came over to the fire and threw the bottle in. Flames shot out straight towards Jon. He was on fire. He was able to put them out by rolling on the ground but was still in intense pain. He knew his burns were bad. He needed to get to a hospital. How was he going to explain this to his parents? How was he going to explain this to his coaches? Was he going to be able to run for the rest of the season? This was bad.

The State Takes Notice

The next day there was no school so the team practiced in the morning. Everyone noticed that Jon was missing. Those that had been with him the night before didn't say anything. The team did their workout, and after practice the varsity went over to Jon's to see what had happened. The doctors ordered him to keep his burns out of the sun for at least two weeks. This meant Jon was not going to be able to practice with the team for that entire span. Despite his performance at the Lyons Township Invite, he had been practicing well and looked as if he would be running in the top five before the season was over. This changed everything. He was going to either have to run very early in the morning or late at night. The team stayed at Jon's house for a little while and then went home. The six of them were going to have to shoulder the responsibility of their success for the mean time.

The team could not dwell on their fallen teammate for too long. They had another invite coming up that Saturday. By the time Friday came around, the mood had lightened on the team. They had been practicing well together, and the previous weekend's race had given them confidence in themselves. Joe's toe felt better, and the rest of the team was feeling healthy and ready to go.

The team boarded the bus earlier than usual on Saturday morning. They had to drive about forty minutes north to get to the Marmion Military Academy Royal Cadet Invitational. This race ran slightly longer than most other races. Most courses were between 2.8 and 3 miles, but Marmion's course was 3.1 miles or 5 kilometers. This didn't worry the Mustangs too much. They all had a good week of practice and felt ready for this race. They got an extra boost of confidence because after looking at how the other teams had performed the week before, Downers South was clearly the best. There were some good individual runners but none of the teams were deep enough to pose a challenge. The previous week the team had warmed up before the race feeling tense and nervous. This week there was a quiet swagger about the six runners. They joked amongst themselves. None of them felt too worried about this race. One of the runners overheard another team boasting about how they were going to easily win the meet. They would soon get a rude awakening.

The runners came to the starting line, did their practice starts, listened to the coaches talk, and lined up to start the race. They joked around and kidded with each other as they waited for the starter to begin the race. Finally, they quieted down as the starter gave instructions and tensely waited for the starting gun.

Bang!

The gun went off. The team ran the first mile in an intimidating pack. All six of them were running together in the top ten. As they approached the second mile Ben and a few other front runners pulled ahead. The Downers South team began to string out. Joe and Devon paired up and ran ahead of the other three who were not far behind. About half way through the race, Devon looked back. He could see nothing but Downers Grove South's blue jerseys. This race was theirs for the taking. They came into the final stretch. Ben barely missed first place by four seconds. There was a gap of four places and then here they came. Devon came in at seventh place, Joe was four seconds behind him in eighth, and Nick four seconds behind him in ninth. Dave and Jeff finished next to each other in eleventh and twelfth places.

Downers South won the meet in a landslide. The next closest team was almost thirty points behind them. Even with a runner missing, the Mustangs still dominated. On the bus ride back the team was exhilarated. They enjoyed their first place finish. They would find out something the next day that would raise their spirits further. The team had climbed from being unranked all the way to twelfth in the state. It was no secret anymore. This team was a force to be reckoned with.

The Mustangs Make a Statement

Every year since 1978 Downers Grove South held the Mustang Invite, an invitational on their home course at O'Brien Park. It consistently showcased many teams that would later go on to State, and this year was no exception. Saint Charles North High School had been building their program up for a few seasons, and this year their work had finally come into fruition. They had one of the top ten teams in the state as well as a runner who was one of the top twenty-five runners in the state. They would be a formidable challenge for the Mustangs.

Facing this team on their home course inspired the Mustangs. They were riding a wave of confidence after their victory at Marmion and wanted to continue their winning ways. The Mustang Invite fell only a week after Marmion, and the varsity could barely wait to show Saint Charles North what they were made of. The runners were also excited to learn that although Jon would not be able to practice with them during the week, the doctors had cleared him to run for the Mustang Invite. They not only wanted to show Saint Charles North that they were a team to be respected, but they also wanted to bring out some of their own fans to support their home team.

Throughout the week the runners told everyone they knew to come to the meet. They told their parents, friends, teachers, relatives, and anyone else that would listen to come out and see that cross country was something worth watching. Even the athletic director, who usually only made appeareances at football and basketball games, came out to see the show. The anticipation around the team and the school grew as the week went on. The team even had an easier workout schedule just to make sure they would put on a good performance for the home fans.

Race day came and the turnout was unbelievable. The Mustang Invite usually didn't bring out many more people outside of the families of the runners that were competing, but today this was truly an event to behold. An hour before the first race started, O'Brien Park was filled with people. Apparently the runners' efforts to create hype had worked because this turnout was unprecedented. As the varsity race drew nearer more people filled the empty space left in the park. They all wanted to see the main event that they had been hearing about all week. They wanted to see a showdown between two of the top teams in state, and they would not be disappointed.

Coach Bicicchi always took the team aside before their races to impart some of his motivation and wisdom on them. He wanted to do something different for an occasion as special as this. Two things that he thought help soldiers going into battle are a flag with their colors and motivational music. Taking this into consideration, he planned out his pre-race speech during the week.

He gathered the seven runners together and started out; "Music always helps to add extra motivation." He then turned on a radio he had situated behind him and epic battle music from a war movie blasted out of the speakers. As he told the team about how they needed to take pride in their home course and represent their team well in front of the home fans, he gave them something else that gave them all an intense injection of pride and adrenaline. He screamed, "Now look at your flag!" He pointed to the top of the hill that sat prominently in the middle of O'Brien Park. A man was waving a Downers Grove South Mustangs Cross Country flag. Coach Bicicchi had bought this flag without telling anyone about it and saved it just for today. As the runners stared in disbelief at their flag flying in the wind, they almost exploded with excitement. He finished his speech; "now honor your flag, honor your school, honor your team, and most of all honor your parents!"

After that exhilarating speech, they felt ready for anything. They could have gone into battle if commanded at that moment. They took the line ready to give all of these people that had come out one hell of a show. The team could barely stand to wait at the line. Two minutes stretched out like two hours. The starter finally had them step to the line. "On your marks…get set…"

Bang!

He fired the gun and the race was off. As they proceeded into their first lap, they saw a huge crowd of people all yelling and cheering for them. The entire football team had come over from their practice to watch the race. They lined a stretch of the course three people deep to cheer on the runners. All around the course fans showed their support and encouraged the home team.

Few people on the team were as excited as Dave and Joe were. They both came into the season with something to prove. Both of them had missed the previous season and wanted to show everyone how good they really were. Ben went out in front as usual but Dave and Joe were not far behind. Devon tried to keep up with them, but he fell behind just after the first mile. Dave and Joe raced against each other now, each periodically pushing the pace. The adrenaline pumping through their veins made it seem as if they would never tire. With about a mile to go, Dave dropped the hammer. He took off from Joe and never looked back. He crossed the line in eighth place. His time was thirty seconds faster than what he had run on this same course at the alumni race just a month ago. Dave had put fifteen seconds between him and Joe in the last mile. Joe still finished in eleventh place with a great time. Jeff had run a statement race, finishing fourth on the team ten seconds behind Joe. Any doubts the team had about Jeff going into the season went away after this race. He had established a strong pace and maintained it the entire race. His time at this race was his personal best at O'Brien Park by more than a minute. Nick and Devon both finished about ten seconds behind Jeff. Jon was in pain from his burns the entire race. He finished seventh on the team well behind Nick and Devon.

Ben meanwhile battled throughout the race with Saint Charles North's first runner. Somewhere around the half-way point of the race, Ben cruised ahead and finished in first place by twenty seconds. It had been quite a few years since a Downers South runner had won the Mustang Invite. Ben's time went for third best ever by a Downers South runner at their home course. The team did not disappoint.

The Mustangs were not able to beat Saint Charles North, but they had given them a run for their money. Saint Charles had not expected any competition entering the race, but they were surprised by this tenacious team. From the gun the race had clearly been between the two schools. The third place team was fifty points behind Downers South. Saint Charles was only able to win by pulling away at the tail end of the race. Once again the Downers Grove South Mustangs had shown the state they were a team to be respected, and they were not going away.

The Team is Almost Caught Sleeping

Two days after the Mustang Invite, Downers South had a dual meet against their conference rival Hinsdale South. A dual meet is a meet run against one other school within the conference. This was an important meet because Hinsdale was their biggest competition in the conference so winning this meet would give them a great chance at finishing in first place. Unfortunately the team had not been thinking about this meet. They had been so focused on the Mustang Invite that they completely disregarded this simple dual meet. That was a mistake because Hinsdale South had shown up ready to run.

Hinsdale had anticipated the Mustangs would have somewhat of an emotional hangover after their big home invite and hoped to take advantage of that. To make things more difficult it was a very humid and muggy day. The air was thick and hard to breathe. One would perspire by just standing outside. This did not help the mentally and physically weary Downers South team. The two teams warmed up and approached the line.

Bang!

The racers were off. Right away, the team could tell they were still fatigued from the race they had just run two days ago. Joe was one of the few runners on the team feeling good so he went out with Ben at the front of the race. Dave ran with Hinsdale's best runner about ten seconds behind Joe and Ben. Devon, Nick, and Jeff were struggling well behind Dave. Jon, still plagued by pain from his burns, trailed behind them. The coaches felt tense after watching the teams go through the first mile. Their team obviously was not feeling sharp today. Hinsdale South ran right alongside Downers South. If the Mustangs didn't start making some moves to win this race, they very well might lose it.

Mid-way through the race Joe could feel something was not right. He labored to breathe, and felt a lot of pain coming from his chest. All of a sudden, something popped underneath his ribcage. It was like he had gotten stabbed in the chest. He couldn't keep pace and fell off sharply from Ben. He would limp his way through the rest of the race. Meanwhile, Dave was still going at it with Hinsdale's top runner, Alex Wright. They flew past the pain-stricken Joe and approached the two-mile mark of the race. These two had been rivals since their freshman year. Both of them had been the best freshman on their teams and immediately got promoted to varsity. Alex had gotten the best of Dave while he had been hurt last year, and Dave was excited to be going at it with his rival once again. With quarter mile left in the race, the two runners were still neck-and-neck. In a sprint, Alex barely beat out Dave in the end. Ben had won, and Dave finished in third. Dave's gutsy race proved crucial. His third place finish was pivotal for the Mustangs because, after him, the team was not looking very good.

Two stand-out sophomores from Hinsdale South had taken fourth and fifth place. Coach Keogh desperately urged on his runners to finish strong. If they didn't start feeling a sense of urgency, they would lose this race. While Joe fell back and Dave was getting ready for an impressive finish, Devon and Jeff felt like they were moving in slow motion. They reached the top of a hill that marked just under a mile to go in the race, and both of them felt like collapsing. The humidity made it impossible for them to draw in a decent breath and each step felt more agonizing than the last. Devon was giving it everything he had just to keep up a modest pace. He slowly pulled ahead of Jeff. In the last half mile, Devon continued to pull ahead and finished just behind Joe in sixth place. Joe collapsed on the ground in pain after crossing the finish line. Another Hinsdale South runner crossed the line in seventh place followed by Jeff in eighth. Nick also had a rough race and finished twenty seconds behind Jeff. Jon finished ten seconds behind Nick. The burns on his arm and face seared with pain. He had never felt this much pain before. His body hurt from running, and his burns felt as if they were on fire again. Sophomore Steve Schmid barely lost to him. They Mustangs had not put on a strong showing today.

Downers South won the meet by only four points. They would not have won without Dave's impressive third place finish. The team breathed a collective sigh of relief as they rode the bus home. That was too close. The coaches knew that kind of performance would not win them conference much less take them to State. That night Coach Keogh and Bicicchi discussed how they wanted to approach the rest of the season. They both agreed on what to do; give these guys hell. The team had three weeks until they ran a significant race. Three weeks to prepare. Three weeks to make seven young men into one team. Three weeks to breed a champion.

Getting the Team Ready for the State Series

The team had almost a month until it had another significant race. The only races they would run in the mean time were dual meets against weaker conference teams. The coaches knew that they needed to get their runners in shape for the State Series. The State Series is a string of four races starting with the Conference Championship race and ending with the State Meet a month later. In between those two races are the Regional Race and the Sectional Race. The top five teams from the Regional move on to the Sectional, and the top five teams from Sectionals advance to State. Illinois was notorious for being one of the most talented states for cross country in the nation. It easily ranked in the top three in depth of talent year in and year out. Most of that talent came out of the Chicago suburbs where Downers Grove South was located. The Mustangs would be competing against these talented suburban teams in their Regional and Sectional, and they would need to be ready. This team was talented but just a tiny slip up in a deep Regional or Sectional could end a team's season.

Coach Keogh and Bicicchi anticipated this and were going to push the top seven to the limit to get them ready for the task that lay ahead. They could not afford another race like the one they had against Hinsdale South. The State Series was too competitive to bring anything less than the team's top performance. From day one after the Hinsdale meet the coaches started cracking the whip. If the team wasn't hammering out interval workouts on the track, they were testing their endurance in long distance runs no shorter than ten miles. An easy day would consist of a fast-paced run lasting for at least an hour.

Joe went to the doctor the day after the Hinsdale race and found out the pain in his chest the day before had been the result of his diaphragm tearing. The diaphragm is a muscle directly underneath the rib cage which helps with breathing. Joe would have to deal with this for the rest of the season if he wanted to continue running. He did not tell anyone about this. He did not want to risk being held out of workouts and races because of something he had no hope of healing before the season was over. He opted to suffer through the pain. This was Joe's last season of high school and nothing would hold him back from reaching his dreams.

The rest of the team was healthy and ready for the work that lay ahead. Jon was back practicing with the team every day, and he was getting back in the shape he had been in before the accident. These weeks of hard work were made easier by the fact that the seven runners were finally coming together as one team. Their success thus far and the challenge of making it to State had given them a common goal to rally around. They were now united by a desire to achieve great things together. Even the most individualistic members of the team started to believe in the great things this team was capable of. Thanks to the constant motivational talks from Coach Bicicchi and the constant encouragement from Coach Keogh, the Mustangs were learning to believe in themselves and trust each other.

They had a dual meet against Morton High School a week after the Hinsdale South meet. It was no contest. Ben, Dave, Joe, and Devon all crossed the line before Morton's first runner. Nick, Jon, and Jeff came in at seventh, eighth, and ninth places. It was encouraging to see Jon running strong in a race for the first time all season. The real story of this race was the top four finishers. Ben made a run at the course record, running by himself the entire time. Dave continued his success, crossing the line as a solid second man on the team once again. Joe, torn diaphragm and all, finished one second shy of his personal best time at O'Brien Park's course. Devon had his best race since Marmion. He shook off a week of feeling slow and fatigued after the Hinsdale South dual meet and recorded his best time at O'Brien Park. The team ran this having not tapered off their training at all. This race was just another workout for them.

A week after Morton was the last race against a conference opponent until the Conference Championship Meet. The Mustangs had trained hard through another week. They were facing Willowbrook High School today. This team had been a State qualifier in previous years, but after losing many seniors the year before; they did not have the depth to compete with Downers South. Both of the teams' top runners sat out the race. Ben was feeling some foot pain and Williowbrook's all-state runner, Jesse Luciano, was having discomfort as well. It was up to the rest of the team's varsity squads to settle this contest.

Even without Ben, the Mustangs still dominated. They took second through tenth place. Devon recorded another strong performance, finishing first on the team in the absence of Ben. The rest of the varsity finished with solid performances as well. They had all but wrapped up Conference and were focusing on two more weeks of training before the Conference Championship Race. Before then, the coaches wanted to take the team somewhere most of them had not been. Coach Keogh and Bicicchi wanted their runners to run on hallowed ground that legends had run on in years past. They wanted the team to see what their goal was. They wanted their team to run at Detweiller.

The Promised Land

Every year, the Illinois State Cross Country Meet was held at Detweiller Park in Peoria. One could not have made a better strip of land for running. The inclines on the hills were just right to speed runners up going down them but to not slow them down while climbing them. It was open enough to fit the thirty teams that ran at State every year. The ground was just the right consistency that sometimes it felt as if it ran the race for you. Detweiller Park was more similar to a track than a cross country course. Legendary runners that would go on to be collegiate All-American and Olympian athletes had run extraordinary times on this course. This is where Coach Keogh and Bicicchi wanted to take their team for a practice.

Early on a cool Saturday morning in early October, the varsity team boarded an old rusty van that the school had spared and made the three hour trip down to Peoria. They slept most of the way down and awoke just in time. The team felt almost giddy with excitement at seeing this course. This was no simple stretch of grass. This was what they had been working towards for the last five months. This is what their coaches screamed at them for motivation through long and arduous workouts. This was the Promised Land.

They got out and stretched their legs. The workout today was simple. They were running three individual miles; fast. They lined up where the starting line would be and pictured standing elbow to elbow with almost three hundred other runners. They pictured the thousands of fans that would be lining the course. They pictured the excitement and anticipation they would feel when the opportunity came.

All of a sudden, Coach Keogh interrupted their lofty thoughts; "ready, set, and go." They were off. They couldn't believe how fast this course was. They didn't even have to try to all run five minutes or under for their first mile. This was exhilarating. They imagined themselves flying through the first mile at State. They started the next mile. This was even faster than the first. It was as if their anticipation to go to this course was pulling them along faster than usual. They weren't even tired as they readied themselves for the last mile. They concluded their workout with their fastest mile yet. It was as if the team had run in unison as one entity.

They were all thinking on the same page. They were all motivated by the same goal. Coach Keogh and Bicicchi knew they finally had a true team on their hands.

On the long ride home the runners and coaches were all thinking the same thing. They weren't thinking about the homecoming dance that night, nor were they thinking about the Conference Championship Race in a week. They thought about the glory and glamour of State. The eyes of the entire state watching their team run together. They felt as if it was their destiny to stand on that starting line in five short weeks. If only they knew what lay ahead of them.

A Dominant Display

There was no school on Monday so the team practiced in the morning. It was a beautiful day, and the top seven felt very optimistic about the approaching State Series. They were fresh off of their workout in Peoria and excited to finally be running significant races again. The Conference Championship was coming up on Saturday, and if the Mustangs won they would take home their first Conference Championship in four years. The team went through a relatively easy week of workouts compared to what they had been doing. The Hinsdale South dual meet still lingered in the back of Coach Keogh's mind, and he was taking no chances this time. He wanted his team to be fit and ready to go out and wrap up Conference. There had been a dispute between Coach Keogh and Coach Bicicchi about how to approach the Conference Championship. Coach Bicicchi insisted that the team was far better than any other team in the conference, and that they could win running backwards. Coach Keogh would have none of that. He was going to ensure that his team had a strong showing at Conference to build their confidence for the State Series.

It was a short bus ride to get to the course that the Conference Meet was being run on. They couldn't have picked a better day to run. It was sixty degrees and sunny. There wasn't a cloud in the sky. It was a perfect autumn day; ideal running weather.

Downers South started out with a strong showing winning both the freshman and sophomore races. These strong performances by the underclassmen made juniors Dave and Devon excited about the team they might be able to field next year. Before they got too wrapped up in looking a year ahead, they needed to take care of business today. The mood was pretty light in the Downers South camp. The varsity team had never felt this confident all year. After their strong performances at the start of the season and the three weeks of tough workouts they had been through, they were excited to see how far they had come.

When the team went out for their warm-up jog, there was a quiet confidence about them. They knew they were the best team out here today. Hinsdale South had been harboring hopes of an upset all week, but they had no idea what they were up against today. This was not the same Downers South team that had barely squeaked out a win a few weeks ago. These were not the same seven nervous and fatigued runners that had raced in the Hinsdale South dual meet. These were well trained athletes who were ready to go out and show what they were capable of. This was a team ready to go out and take what was theirs.

The coaches led their runners in some practice starts and gave them their pre-race speech. They were ready. Bring it on. As they stood at the line the runners were getting excited and pumping each other up. They just wanted that gun to sound to set them loose on their unsuspecting opponents.

Bang!

The race was under way. After the first quarter mile, it was all Mustangs. Willowbrook's Jesse Luciano and Ben took the lead followed by an unlikely competitor. A promising sophomore from Hinsdale South had a little too much confidence and tried to keep pace with the two front runners. He had run a strong race at Peoria but that course was made for speed. The course today would not produce the same times as Detweiller Park. After about a mile, the sophomore from Hinsdale dropped back never to recover.

As Ben and Luciano took control of the race and the overconfident sophomore from Hinsdale quickly fell behind, the rest of the runners were getting comfortable. Dave's rival, Alex Wright, made a move and went ahead of the pack that formed behind the two leaders. Behind him a group consisting of Devon, Joe, Dave, and another sophomore from Hinsdale South ran strongly. Devon had not felt this good in a race all year; he felt as if he could run all day. Joe fought through his torn diaphragm and kept pace with his teammate. Dave did not feel as fresh as his teammates today. He did not have the same energy that had carried him to strong finishes all season. He struggled to keep pace with Joe and Devon. Behind them Jeff, Nick, and Jon ran a solid pace together around tenth place. Half-way through the race the Mustangs were running away with it. They only needed to finish, and the Conference Championship would be theirs.

Ben ran strongly in second place, and he would cross the line with a very strong three mile time of 15:22. He paced with Luciano until the Willowbrook runner pulled away for the win. Ben did not expect to beat the far superior Luciano and was satisfied with his second straight second place finish in Conference. As they neared a mile to go in the race, Devon and another sophomore from Hinsdale were putting some distance between them and Dave and Joe. They approached a hill that marked exactly one mile left in the race, and Devon knew this was his chance to make a move. This was the same hill that he, Joe, and Dave had practiced on every Saturday at York Camp. He had run up this hill hundreds of times, and this time would be his best yet. He surged up the hundred meter long hill. By the time he had gone down the other side, the sophomore from Hinsdale had fallen far behind. Devon was in fourth place by himself now, and he could see Alex Wright running not too far ahead of him. He set his eyes on his target and went for it. With about half a mile to go, he ran down another hill and leaped over a creek. He was gaining ground fast. He could hear some voices urging him to catch up to Alex before it was too late. As he approached the last quarter mile of the race, he pulled even with his competitor. The two went hard down a gradual decline and approached the final one hundred meters run uphill. Devon thought back over all his hard work and the pain that he had gone through to get to this point. It wasn't enough. Alex pulled ahead in a sprint and beat him by four seconds. It didn't matter that he had lost out on third place. Devon had just run his best time that season by almost twenty seconds. Last year, Alex had been more than a minute faster than him. He was very happy about his race. After catching his breath after crossing the finish line he looked back to watch the rest of his team finish the race.

Joe and Dave pulled each other through the last mile of the race. Joe's chest was killing him, and Dave just did not have his legs under him today. Regardless, they pressed on through their ailments. A runner from Morton caught up to them with a quarter mile to go. They would have none of that. They dropped the hammer and left him flailing behind them. Joe and Dave crossed the finish line at sixth and seventh place. Jeff and Nick came across three seconds behind them. Six out of the top ten runners wore Downers Grove South jerseys. As Jon crossed the line in thirteenth place, the domination was complete. The Mustangs were champions.

Smiles were stuck on everyone's faces. The team stood at the awards ceremony and received their trophy with a tremendous sense of pride. They knew they had earned this victory. They overcame a lot to get to this point. Many of the other coaches remarked to Coach Keogh and Bicicchi that this was one of the strongest teams they had ever seen come out of this Conference. No one had anticipated they would be this good. The state took notice too. Since the Mustangs had not run in an invite in a month they had slipped in the rankings. After their performance at Conference, they were moved back up to thirteenth in the rankings; their highest ranking since they had won the Marmion Invite. The team joyously celebrated together that night. A team united in victory. They could not dwell on this for long though. There was still work to be done.

Legendary

The next meet after the Conference Championship was Regionals. The Regional Race could be easy or hard depending on where a school was located. Downers South was located in an area containing most of the best running programs in the state. The Regional they were going to was by far the most difficult one in the state. In fact, it was the most difficult Regional the state had ever seen. The top five teams advanced, but the sixth, seventh, and eighth place teams would make it through any other Regional in the state. The competition was so good that the span of one second would be two or three places in the race. Hearts would be broken at this race. Many runners that deserved to move on to the next round would be going home instead. This was the lion's den that the Mustangs headed into.

The practices were lighter this week than they had been the last. Towards the end of the week, the coaches gave their team daily speeches to mentally prepare them for the race on Saturday. They had something else in store that would give their team an extra shot of confidence. A few weeks earlier Coach Bicicchi had gotten the idea to order the team new uniforms for the State Series. He believed that to run like a champion one needed to be dressed like one. He wanted his runners to feel like they were better than the runner next to them. He wanted them to feel like men headed into an epic conflict. He had ordered the lightest most comfortable fabric he could find and picked out an exciting new design to get his men fired up.

The team arrived at the usual team dinner held on Friday evening before a Saturday race. As the runners came in, they noticed something that was covered up in the front room. They wondered throughout dinner what might be hidden in there. After they finished their meals the coaches called them into the front room. Coach Bicicchi spoke to them; "In order to perform like a champion one needs to be dressed like a champion. When you guys are out there against the toughest competition in the state, I want you to be able to spot each other out at any point during the race. You need to stand out from the rest of the crowd. You need to stand out to people because your performance will make it impossible to ignore you." With those words he revealed what was being hidden.

Coach Bicicchi revealed seven powder blue uniforms hanging up neatly in a row. The runners could not believe their eyes. The only new equipment this team had received recently were extra warm up sweats that the girls team didn't need. They were not used to getting anything special because they had not been anything special. These uniforms were something special for a special team. When they tried on the uniforms, the fabric was so light and soft it felt as if they weren't wearing anything at all. They stood together and glanced back and forth at each other. No one could take the smiles off of their faces. They were all thinking the same thing. They could not wait to show off their brand new prizes tomorrow. They couldn't wait to show themselves off tomorrow. What a show it would be.

The Regional would be held at the same course the Conference Championship Race had been held. The team arrived plenty early to set up camp and relax before the race. Many runners lay down and listened to music on their ipods. A few joked around, trying to keep their moods light. Devon lay against a tree reading a book. He had a look of total concentration on his face. After his long awaited break-out performance the week before at the Conference Championship, he could not wait to go out on this same course and see what he could do today.

Ben lay down, resting his head on his duffle bag, and planning out his race. This was his shot to make a run at being all-state. He knew the competition would be tough, but he decided he would try to win this race today. He had cruised to a strong finish at Conference and felt completely rested and ready for this race. His chances to win were very good. The teams were good and very deep with talent, and he could run with the best individuals each of these teams had to offer. Ben was one of maybe four or five that had an actual chance at winning. He calmly awaited his opportunity.

Joe had an intense look of determination on his face as he laced up his racing spikes. He knew his chest would be in pain from the gun, and he was ready for it. Nothing could stop him today. He was prepared to go to any length to score points for his team and help them advance to the Sectional Meet a week later. Dave stretched out his sore hamstring and planned out his race. He would not let himself fall behind like he had at Conference. If Devon was going to try and go ahead again, Dave wanted to be right by his side. The two had been running together for almost a year now and Dave did not want to let his running partner get away from him in this race. He tried to keep his calm as he started to take off his warm-up sweats.

Jeff had a look of confidence on his face. He had performed well last week and knew he had more in him. This was his chance to really step up and score some points for his team. This was his chance to make everyone forget about his subpar summer training. He was feeling ready to wear his new uniform with pride and have a great performance today. Nick tried to quell a nervousness that had been bothering him all morning. His chest felt tense. His throat was tightening up and making it hard to swallow. As the team set out on their warm-up jog Nick was trying to get in a good place mentally and think positive thoughts about the upcoming race. Jon felt ready for the first time all season. He had been hampered by one thing after another, but today he felt ready to run. He excitedly hopped on the balls of his feet as the team approached the starting line. He couldn't wait to get out there.

The team did their practice starts and huddled around the coaches. Coach Bicicchi's message was simple and clear: "We're here. Let's show everyone we have arrived and that we're not going anywhere!" The team could barely stand still at the line. This was the big stage. They were lining up next to all-state runners and some of the most elite teams in the state. They had not faced many of these teams all season. They could not wait to show these new opponents who they were.

The starter spoke through a microphone. The wait before these races was longer than usual because the starter had to go over rules and starting procedure. Every little detail was laid out and made clear. After informing the anxious runners of the rules and expectations the final procedure began. "Runners step to the line...now take yours marks;" the wait between each command was unbearable. The several seconds between each one drew out like hours. "Get set;" the runners and the entire crowd held their breath.

Bang!

The race was off. The challenge at the beginning of these ultra competitive races was establishing position in the race. If one started out too slowly, they would be too far back and spend the entire race playing catch-up. In a race like this where each place was so crucial, that was a mistake a runner could not afford to make. All eighty-four runners funneled together as the beginning of the race quickly went into a tight space between two groups of trees. Ben was near the front right away. He wanted to establish his position with the leaders. Dave and Joe were together around twentieth place. The adrenaline pumped through their veins and helped them get out to a strong start. This race was so fast, and there were so many runners around them, that they were carried to a faster start than they were used to. Devon was waiting back. He was not gifted with a lot of natural quickness. His racing strategy was outlasting people, and he did not want to start out faster than he was ready for. He sat about eight places behind Joe and Dave, slowly working his way up. He felt supremely confident, and was not worried in the least that he was behind Joe and Dave so early. Jeff, Jon, and Nick ran together a few places behind Devon. They were working together, taking turns leading and pushing the pace. A half mile into the race, the Mustangs had good early position.

Approaching the mile, Ben kept pace with three other runners at the front of the race. All of a sudden someone caught his foot, and he went down hard. Many times a runner's race can be ruined after getting tripped up. Their focus is broken, and they become rattled and are unable to regain their pace. Ben was not letting that happen. He kept his cool, immediately got back up, and fell in with the other three runners at the front of the race. He was bound and determined to make a statement that he was one of the state's best runners. A little trip up was a minor obstacle he had to overcome. The lead runners flew through the mile with Ben tucked right in with them. He was not going anywhere.

Devon had caught up to Joe and Dave about three quarters of a mile into the race. He had never felt so focused and relaxed in a race before. His mindset was so positive and confident that he was tempted to crack a joke to his teammates. He opted instead to stay focused on the race. Dave felt much better today than he had the previous week. He had a strong pace established and felt comfortable with it. He felt ready to take on the next two miles. Joe was not in as good of shape. His chest pain was unbearable, and it hadn't even been a mile. He just couldn't breathe. As Devon and Dave cruised through the mile, Joe began to fall back.

Coach Keogh and Bicicchi could not believe their eyes. After seeing their first four runners go through the mile in under five minutes, Jeff, Jon, and Nick raced by them just a few seconds over five minutes. Their team looked great early on. The coaches ran to the other side of the course to catch them coming around the far side.

As Jon, Jeff, and Nick started their second mile, Jeff took the lead and started putting space between him and the two others. He was feeling great and wanted to catch up to Joe, Dave, and Devon. He stretched out his long legs and started gaining speed. He had good reason to feel confident before the race. He just ran a 5:02 mile as easily and gracefully as if he were going for a brisk jog. He felt great. During the second mile Jeff caught up to Joe and dragged him along. He wasn't letting his friend fall behind. He kept encouraging Joe and wouldn't let him leave his side. These two were in this race together and nothing was going to hold them back.

Not far behind them, Jon and Nick were still running very well. They were the last two runners on the team and were still in the top forty places in the race. As Nick began to tire, Jon set the pace and pulled Nick along with him. Jon finally had his opportunity to step up. The entire season had been an uphill battle for him. Today he was reaching the peak of that climb. He couldn't remember the last time his legs felt this quick. This course was truly a cross country course with rolling hills and a jump over a creek. Usually, Jon did not perform as well on courses like these, but today was not the usual. He powered up the hills, flew down the other side, and strongly hurdled over the creek. It felt as if a weight that had been sitting on his shoulders all season was finally lifted. Jon felt as if he was gaining momentum with every step.

At the front of the race, the leaders started to separate themselves from the rest of the pack. Flying through the two-mile, the top three runners continued to quicken their pace. The other two runners made a move and Ben went with them, but he couldn't hold the pace. Ben had never been a short distance sprinter, and the first two runners definitely had that advantage on him. They pulled away with a quarter mile to go. The top two had a great finish, crossing the line neck-and-neck. Ben came through in third at 15:07 for three miles. He had not done too bad for being underrated coming into the race and getting tripped up at the mile. His time was fifteen seconds faster than the week before on this course. He caught his breath and anxiously looked back to see how the rest of the team was doing.

Dave and Devon had pulled ahead of Joe and ran most of the second mile together. As Devon glanced at the clock stationed at the two mile marker he couldn't believe his eyes. It read 10:26. His previous fastest time for any single two mile race had been 10:33. He had clocked a personal best time for the first mile as well. This was unbelievable, but his race was not over yet. He had a mile to go and was determined to make it the best one yet. He sprinted up the hill just after the two mile marker. Dave fought to keep up. Dave was running very well, but Devon just kept speeding up. After two miles, he was just getting warmed up. As the two approached the downhill before the jump over the creek, Dave managed to catch up to Devon one last time. That was the last time he would see him for the rest of the race.

As Devon sped down the hill, he could see Hinsdale South's Alex Wright a few places ahead of him. Devon hurdled over the creek and surged to catch up to the group Alex was running with. The pack rounded the top of the hill that marked a quarter mile to go, and Devon made his move. As he moved to the front of the pack he saw Coach Keogh to his right. Coach Keogh frantically shouted at him to finish strong. As the pack approached the last hundred meters uphill, they gave it everything they had. A few people passed Devon, but he still held his own. He crossed the line and the clock read 15:40. That was sixteen seconds faster than he had run on this same course the previous week. That was more than thirty seconds faster than his fastest time on a three mile course had been two weeks ago. He couldn't believe what had just happened. He just recorded his best times for the mile, two mile, and three mile all in one race.

He quickly composed himself. He couldn't celebrate yet. There were still five of his teammates out there.

With a half mile left to go Joe was in excruciating pain. How could he endure anymore of this? Jeff had almost literally dragged him through the last mile of the race. Joe was hoping he would just be able to finish the race, much less turn it on for a strong kick. Then he saw his older brother off to the side of the course. His brother was just as passionate as their father was, and he screamed like a mad man to encourage his little brother. That was all Joe needed to hear. He wasn't going to let his big brother and his teammates down. He pushed through the pain and sped up dramatically with Jeff right at his side. The two caught up with Dave and pulled him right along with them. They were passing up runners left and right. Joe, Jeff, and Dave were jostling for position to lead the trio. With two hundred meters to go Joe took the lead with his teammates hot on his tail. Joe, Jeff, and Dave crossed the finish line all in a row. All three had bettered their time from the week before by at least fifteen seconds. That was it right there. They had just secured the Mustangs' dominating performance.

Jon was setting the pace followed closely by Nick. With just under a half mile to go, he turned it on. He was a half mile runner in track, and he used this speed to his advantage.

Nick tried to keep up, but he couldn't match Jon's quickness. Jon ran against everything that had been holding him back all season. He ran against his anxiety that had caused him to run poorly in the first race. He ran against the terrible accident that held him out of practice for two weeks. He ran against those that had doubted him and suggested bringing sophomore Steve Schmid up to varsity. Today he triumphed over all of it. He crossed the line twelve seconds faster than he had run the week before. Jon had proven to himself, and to everyone else, that he was not down for the count just yet. He could have mailed it in a long time ago and let the rest of the team have their success. Today was his reward for the adversity he had faced throughout the season. As Nick finished three seconds behind Jon, it was complete.

Joe had collapsed on the ground in pain, and his teammates dog piled on top of him in joy. The team was ecstatic. The Mustangs owned the day. As the other coaches checked the scores they couldn't believe what they were seeing. Even Coach Keogh and Bicicchi couldn't believe what they were seeing. Downers South had gone into the hardest Regional in the state and taken a commanding third place. They had come out and made a statement. They had arrived.

The local papers raved about their Cinderella team. They glorified the Mustangs as a hungry up-and-coming team led by their undaunted first runner. Much fuss was made in the papers of Ben's gutsy performance after getting tripped up early in the race. The state rankings moved the Mustangs up to twelfth, matching their highest ranking all year. They were quoted in saying "the Mustangs are probably taking numbers of observers eating crow after they finished a strong third at the Hinsdale Central Regional, which is considered the toughest in the state this year. Many didn't think the Mustangs deserved such a lofty ranking but the truth is they have competed well all season long no matter the competition." Downers South was dubbed "the surprise team of the year". They only needed to place in the top five at the Sectional next week in order to make it to State. Unfortunately for the Mustangs sometimes dreams don't fully come into fruition.

So Close

The Regional had been the toughest in state history, and the Sectional only got harder. The Sectional picked up two other teams that could qualify for State. This meant there would be seven teams all capable of qualifying for State. These seven teams would be running for their lives at the Sectional in order to try and make it through. To make things even more difficult, for the first time all season, the Mustangs had a target on their backs. They no longer had the luxury of sneaking up on teams. The team was not thinking about this though. They were still basking in the glory of their excellent performance at Regionals.

As the team came to practice after school on Monday afternoon the mood was light in the locker room. They were all riding on an incredible wave of momentum that they believed would carry them through the Sectional and on to glory at the State Meet a week later. No one wanted this team to go to State more than Coach Keogh. Throughout his long coaching tenure he had seen many of his teams make it to the Sectional and finish just a place or two off of qualifying for State. This team was the best he had ever coached, and his heart was set on bringing all seven of these runners to the Promised Land.

Coach Bicicchi and Coach Keogh were at odds over how to mentally prepare their runners for the upcoming Sectional Race. Coach Keogh insisted on keeping the mood light and their spirits high. He was worried the team might worry themselves right out of the State Series if too much pressure was placed on their shoulders this week. Coach Bicicchi knew this team was going into the snake pit on Saturday. They needed to be ready to run the race of their lives. Last week had been great, but there was no doubt in his mind that they could have advanced through the Regional. The Sectional would not be so forgiving. Regionals had been very deep and very competitive, but the Sectional was almost twice as big with twice as many runners to break up the Mustangs' devastating pack. As the head coach, Keogh had the final say, and he stuck to his decision to make sure the team did not worry too much during practice that week.

They ran a mile and half time trial on Monday just to get their legs moving and keep them sharp. This would be the only workout for the week. Everything seemed normal as the coaches watched the time trial except Devon lagged in the far rear. He hadn't run this slowly in a workout all season. When they asked him about it after practice he dismissed it as nothing but still feeling a little fatigued from Saturday's race. The rest of the team looked sharp and ready for the upcoming weekend. During the week, the team borrowed a van from the school and went to the Sectional course. While doing some sprints down the final stretch of the race, Devon again noticed that his legs felt slow. He had a funny feeling like something was wrong. He couldn't shake off the thought that something bad was about to happen.

The team boarded the bus on Saturday morning. They were each proudly donning their brand new power blue jerseys that had brought them so much success a week earlier. They hoped their fortunes would continue. When they arrived at the course the team stepped out into another perfect day for running. The last few weeks had been perfect running weather, and today continued this streak of great weather. As they set up camp and relaxed before they started their warm-ups, something was different about them. That buzz and excitement that had surrounded them most of the season was not there. The coaches could tell. They dismissed it as simply jitters before the big race. The team and the two coaches warmed up together and got ready for the big race.

The coaches addressed the runners before they left them at the line. The message they had been stressing all week was only three more miles; only three more miles between them and the State Meet. Compared to the hundreds upon thousands of miles they had run in their lives, three miles was nothing. The coaches said some parting comments and left their team at the starting line. The seven of them huddled up to encourage each other and try to shake off the anxiety they all felt. For once, Devon was not one of the louder voices. He felt something that he could not put his finger on. As the team broke huddle and ran back to the line, Devon felt vulnerable and scared at the start of the race for the first time all year. He felt as if he was at the end of something. Like there was some terrible force at work that he had no control over.

Bang!

The starter fired the gun and the runners were off; only three more miles to go. Early on, the Mustangs got pushed back. Just after the start, there was a sharp u-turn the entire race had to make. Getting almost two hundred people still running in one large pack at full speed to make a one hundred-eighty degree turn was something that was impossible to do smoothly. Downers South came out of this turn having been caught behind. The coaches had warned them about this, but it was no use. Coming out of the turn they had to play catch up for the first mile just to get close to the positions they should be in.

Ben ran at the front of the race as usual. There were more contenders at the front this week, but he still kept pace with them. His chances of winning today were not as good as they had been at the Regional. Nevertheless, he was going for the best position he could get. His team depended on him to score some low points at the front of this race, and he was going to do his best to not let them down.

Further back Dave took the initiative in pulling his teammates along behind him in order the get into the positions they should be in. Jeff ran next to him with Nick bringing up the rear. After two disappointing performances for Dave, today was his opportunity to redeem himself. He had been focused all week on not letting himself fall behind like he had in the Conference and Regional Meets. Dave was up to the task today. Single-handedly, he would make sure the Mustangs would not fall behind in this race. He ran as if his life depended on it today.

Joe, Jon, and Devon were about fifteen seconds behind Dave, Jeff, and Nick. Joe's diaphragm was in constant pain as usual. His strategy to combat that was to not go out as fast as he was used to in order to delay the worst pain for the end of the race. He wanted his urgency to finish the race strong to outweigh the intense pain he would undoubtedly be feeling. Jon fell in next to Joe. He wanted to match his impressive performance from the week before, but he could tell right away he just didn't have it today. His legs weren't feeling as strong as they had at Regionals. He was just trying to hang on for as long as he could. Devon felt like he was running in slow motion. It was like he was stuck in some terrible dream that he couldn't awaken from. He felt no urgency or determination like he was used to feeling during races. He couldn't make any sense of it. As he watched Joe put on a speed burst half-way through the race, he felt powerless to follow him. What was wrong?

At the front of the race, the top three runners had distanced themselves from Ben and a few others. Ben still tucked in firmly around fifth place. As the runners flew through the last mile, Ben battled with the first runner from Benet Academy. Benet had only finished four points behind Downers South at Regionals, and they had been gunning for the Mustangs all week. In the final quarter mile, Benet's first runner and Ben were still battling for fifth place. Benet's first runner opened up his stride and went into a vicious sprint to finish two seconds ahead of Ben. Ben still had finished in sixth place. He looked back and waited longer than he would have liked until he saw the Mustangs' next finisher.

Dave had answered the call today. On a slower course, he came to close to matching his time from the week before. Joe had caught up with him, Jeff, and Nick, but it would not be Joe pulling his teammates along this day. Dave was exhausted, but he still pressed on. With a half mile to go, he dug deep for anything he had left and finished strongly. He left his teammates behind and finished at 16:00; three seconds ahead of Joe and Jeff. Nick finished two seconds behind them. Through five finishers the Mustangs looked strong, but the coaches worried as they watched from the sidelines. They were not sure if this would be good enough. They worried as they watched the last two finishers cross the line.

Devon could not be doing this bad if he had run the race backwards, and he knew it. He put on a weak sprint with a quarter mile to go to come across at 16:10. He had not run this slowly since the first race of the year. This was thirty seconds slower than he had run at Regionals. He turned around to see Jon come across about ten seconds behind him. He hoped and prayed his teammates had taken care of business.

How Could This Have Happened?

As the team cooled down and headed over to the awards ceremony, the mood was grim. The coaches knew it and all but the most hopeful of the top seven knew it. The season was over. They hadn't come up big when they needed to. Despite a somewhat strong performance, it still wasn't good enough. This race required an excellent performance, and that was not what the Mustangs had put on. One could have heard a pin drop at the team's camp as they sat and watched the awards ceremony.

First, the individual State Qualifiers were announced. Ben was one of them. That made it official. Any hope that had been clung to had now been extinguished from their hearts. As they watched the qualifying teams get called up, they all hung their heads low. Devon buried his face in his hat. He felt so ashamed. He couldn't even bear to look at anyone. All of a sudden, an image popped into his head: It was Joe, Dave, and him running together in the hot sun at York Camp. This was too much. He began to cry. He hadn't cried in years, but this was more than he could bear. He had never worked so hard or believed in something so much, and at the end, he felt as if there was nothing to show for it.

Dave was equally as devastated. He looked back for someone, anyone that could offer him some comfort. All he saw was Devon bawling his eyes out. That did it for him. Dave cried too. Everything he and Devon had been working towards for more than a year was gone in the blink of an eye. As the team limped back to the bus, it felt like it took forever. Nothing was said the entire ride back. Dave and Devon couldn't stop crying. Jon looked towards the front of the bus and saw a tear fall down Coach Keogh's cheek. Those that did not cry did so because they were too shocked to know what to feel. These proud men that had overcome the odds were now left with nothing. Ben had qualified for State, but this was not how he wanted it to be. There was only one thing on all of their minds. How could this have happened? They had believed all season that they would reach the goal of making it to the State Meet. They had all dreamed this same dream. They had overcome so much in order to accomplish this. They felt as if it had been their destiny to make it to the Promised Land. What now?

The forty minute bus ride back to school felt like a lifetime. As everyone composed themselves, Coach Bicicchi said a few words to try and cheer them up. As they all straggled off one by one, Dave, Devon, and Jon were the last ones left behind. They sat silently on the trunk of Jon's car for a few minutes and then Dave and Jon heard something. It was Devon. It sounded like someone had just stabbed him. The girls team on the other side of the parking lot heard this and looked over to see where the terrible noise had come from. His voice was soon joined by Dave and Jon's. They were going berserk. Devon had smashed his water bottle on the cement and now was trying to rip the letters off of his letterman jacket. Dave and Jon were in Jon's car running over their shoes. They were all yelling and cursing trying to scare away their pain. They felt robbed. Their hopes and dreams had been taken away from them, and there was nothing they could do about it.

Their parents worried about their sons and for good reason. These had been proud and strong men at the start of the day. It was pitiful how different things were in just a few hours. All day they had sat and brooded alone with nothing but their negative thoughts and never-ending questions to occupy their heads.

Nick met up with Joe, Jon, Dave, and Devon later that night and couldn't believe what he saw. His teammates were a wreck. The four of them could barely speak. They could hardly be recognized as the same people he had been known all season.

Nick quickly went home. He couldn't see his friends like this. The four of them woke up the next morning feeling worse than ever. They all solemnly knew what they needed to do now. They knew it was time to move on. They knew the unbelievable ride was over. They knew the dream was gone.

What Now?

The Friday after the Sectional, the team went down to Peoria to watch Ben run in the State Meet the next day. They were still very upset about their early exit from the State Series the week before, and this was the first time they had all been together since then. This was the first chance they all had gotten to talk with each other about what had just happened. Jon drove Dave and Devon down to Peoria, and the whole ride down they vented their frustrations. They wanted to lash out against something, anything, but there was nothing they could do but swallow their anger and move on.

That night Jon, Jeff, Dave, Devon, and Joe all hung out in one of their hotel rooms that had been rented in anticipation of the team making it to State. They stayed up late into the night. There was much to talk about. They couldn't get over how cheated they felt. They deserved to be here more than most of the rest of the teams that had qualified. Had they not worked as hard as any other team in the state? What was their reward for everything they had endured together? There were teams that qualified out of the less talented sectionals from down-state that didn't have one runner that would come close to running on Downers South's top seven. How was it fair that they had the chance to run tomorrow and the Mustangs didn't?

The next day Nick, Jeff, Joe, Jon, Dave, and Devon watched Ben run. He finished just a couple places shy of all-state. As they all congratulated Ben, they didn't realize this was the last time they would all be together outside of practices. As they parted ways and drove home, some of them would part ways for good. Over the winter months leading into track, some dealt with the disappointment at Sectionals worse than others. Joe, Jeff, Dave, Ben, and Nick would continue to train hard in preparation for track. Jon felt completely mentally and physically burnt out as he drove back home from Peoria. He had put a lot of effort into running over his high school career but felt he didn't have much to show for it. He had already committed to a college and was not planning on competing after high school so running took a backseat in Jon's life.

Devon continued to bear the weight of what had happened at Sectionals on his shoulders. He felt responsible for denying the four other seniors on varsity a chance to run at State. He allowed his guilt and shame to overrule his better judgment and stopped running. Devon inflated his ego to compensate for his hurt pride. This strong leader became a follower. He chose to follow the easy path. Anything was better than dealing with the shame that he felt due to his poor performance.

After everything they had been through together, in the end, the team let their differences come between them once again. Without a common goal to unify them, they went their separate ways. By the time the track season started three months later, some felt like strangers to each other after they had embraced each other as brothers during the fall. The seven of them broke off into their own groups. The pain and shock of falling short of their dreams had been too much to overcome. Ben and Nick went in their own direction. Jeff went in his. Dave, Joe, and Jon would still remain close. Devon seemed to be lost. The magic was gone. At the end of their incredible journey together, it would be seen as an amazing feat that was ultimately too good to be true.

Bringing Devon Back

It was 3:30 in the morning. Devon had been lying awake in bed for the last four hours. He rarely slept well anymore. For the last two months Devon's life had been going in a downward spiral. His grades were dropping, he had been getting into trouble, and he most certainly had not been running. As he lay awake for most of the night in bed, he went over the destructive direction he had been going in. He knew he couldn't continue on like this. He had lost the respect of his friends on the team. They didn't even recognize him anymore. He had been a passionate and inspirational figure on the team. He was always optimistic and excited about working hard and helping his teammates improve. Now, he was just a negative person to be around. He wasn't able to put it all behind him and move on.

After getting a couple hours of sleep, he awoke the next morning and knew something needed to change. He couldn't go on like this. He was miserable and felt his life was spiraling out of control. Something needed to be done, but he didn't know what. He had dug himself into a pretty deep hole and did not know how he would pull himself out of it. He knew he couldn't do this by himself. He needed someone's help. Immediately, he knew exactly who to talk to.

He swallowed his pride and called Coach Bicicchi the next day. Devon looked up to Coach Bicicchi very much. His motivational speeches had always lit a fire under him. Tonight, he needed a motivational talk more than ever. Devon spoke to him over the phone and his coach invited him over, calmly reassuring him; "my home is your home." As Devon pulled into Glenn Bicicchi's driveway he didn't know what to expect. He timidly approached the front door and rang the bell. He came inside and sat with Joe and his coach. Devon began to lay it all out for them.

Devon explained how he felt like he had lost his motivation for running. Despite knowing that he needed to work hard to continue his success and be a leader for next year, he felt helpless to do so. He told them that his guilt after the Sectional had been so powerful that it prompted him to consider quitting the team and give up on running. Glenn knew exactly what to say. He gave Devon a much needed boost of confidence reminding him that it had been him who had been instrumental in helping the team to great success at Conference and Regionals. He explained to Devon that the body is a machine and that eventually either the mental or the physical part breaks down. Coming over for advice tonight was only a sign that the fire that felt like it had all but burnt out was igniting again. He assured Devon that by the end of his senior year he would have run at the State Meet and run 9:40 for two miles in track. Devon, Glenn, and Joe talked for hours. As Devon was getting ready to leave Glenn gave him a hug. He told him to enjoy one more day off because after that he would begin to reaffirm himself as a team leader and dominant runner in the state.

As Devon drove home he felt immense relief. The weight of the guilt and shame he had been carrying around for two months was finally lightened, but he would not let it go just yet. This was to be the kindling that would fuel a roaring fire. He could not wait to begin his trek on the comeback trail. He knew he had missed a lot of time and had fallen behind, but he was determined to make up the ground he had lost.

For almost an entire year after that, the disappointment at the Sectional was no longer something that would bring him down. Devon turned it into an insatiable desire to reach even greater feats than he had achieved last season. Devon would not allow himself to rest until he had avenged what had happened. He would not allow himself to feel as scared and unprepared as he had felt before the Sectional ever again. He was going to prepare himself, and the rest of the team, for what lay ahead. He swore they would not suffer the same fate of the previous fall's team. Devon was back.

Building up for Next Fall

Devon and Dave were the top two runners that would be returning next year. It would be up to them to not only be the leading runners on the team but also to recruit members for next year's varsity team. They had a pretty talented sophomore class. Their sophomores had won Conference and had the top two individual finishers. Sophomore Steve Schmid had even made a run at making varsity for part of the season. Devon and Dave ran together almost every day and would often talk of who might make the team for next year. They were both determined to build another successful team for the fall cross country season. They weren't satisfied to only succeed themselves. They wanted to share the experience of being on a great team with the members that would be on varsity next year.

During the track season Coach Keogh and Coach Bicicchi already knew Devon and Dave would be the captains for next year. They were by far the best returners and no one could match their intensity and desire to compete. They were good friends that worked well together. Together they would try to build a team to match the greatness of the team they had been a part of the previous fall. During the track season, they encouraged the younger runners and would speak with them about doing York Camp over the summer. Devon and Dave both knew they would be returning there, and wanted to bring as many people as possible.

During the track season, Dave looked like he was ready to step up as a team leader for next year. He was running very well. He, Joe, Jeff, and Jon were on one of the best 3200 meter relay teams in the state. Dave enjoyed great individual success in the mile and two-mile races as well. Dave had performed far below his standards while being injured during the entire track season the year before, but this season erased all of those memories.

Devon was feeling the effects of losing two months of running. He had never been a great track runner, and it didn't help that he had come into the season out of shape. The entire indoor and outdoor track season would be an uphill battle for Devon. Despite his lack of success, he continued to work hard in preparation for cross country. He began lifting weights to supplement his running. He wanted every advantage possible over his competition in the fall. He might not be the best runner in the state, but he was sure as hell going to be the most prepared.

A Melancholy Conclusion

The five seniors that were on varsity in cross country started out the track season strong. They were all the top athletes in the long distance events. Ben was one of the top runners in the state for the 3200 meter (two mile) run. Joe was the team's best 1600 meter (mile) runner and had hopes of making it to State in the outdoor season. Jeff was the team's best 800 meter (half-mile) runner and the strongest leg of the 3200 meter relay. Jon, Joe, and Jeff made up three-fourths of the 3200 meter relay which was one of the best in the state. The seniors helped Downers South to have the most dominating distance team in the Conference.

After a strong indoor season, the seniors' success would not continue in outdoor track. Joe had seriously injured his hip during his sophomore year, and he aggravated this old injury running the tight turns on indoor tracks. He would not run another race after indoor track. Jeff and Jon both developed stress fractures during indoor track that would sideline them almost the entire outdoor season. Neither of them would run until the very end of outdoor track. With only Dave remaining, the dominant 3200 meter relay team was no more. Nick would run throughout the entire season but did not train as hard as he had during cross country. He would post good times but never regain his speed from the cross country season.

Ben was the only senior to have a successful outdoor track season. He would qualify for the State Meet in spring. He and Nick both received full scholarships to run for a small private college next year. Jeff and Jon came back to run the outdoor track Conference Championship Meet but would never run competitively after high school. Joe would not run for a few months due to his injury but would come back to help out his father coach the team in the fall.

The track season was over and sun had set on the high school careers of these five seniors. Next season's cross country team was going to require a lot of work to even come close to achieving the kind of success the previous season's team had experienced. The varsity team was losing five of its seven runners. The five runners it lost weren't easily replaceable either. These were five men who possessed an uncommon combination of natural ability and work ethic. As Devon and Dave began to see the candidates that would make up next season's team, they knew they had their work cut out for them. This would be no easy task.

Preparing for the Summer

Throughout the track season, Dave and Devon had been recruiting the runners that showed the potential to be able to compete for the varsity team. At the end of the track season they had assembled a group of six other runners who were willing to train with them at York Camp over the summer.

Steve Schmid was the most promising candidate. He had been close to making varsity the previous season and had come back with a very impressive track season. He was one of the top sophomores in the state during track. He had run varsity in the 3200 meter run almost the entire season. His performances in the mile were equally impressive. What was really impressive about him is that he had a work ethic to match his amazing natural abilities. He trained alongside Dave and Devon all season. Steve was excited to begin his summer training, and even had a shot at competing with Dave and Devon for the top spot on the team.

Sophomore Chris Lechner had been the second best sophomore since cross country. In cross country he had always finished close behind Steve. He had been a very successful 1600 meter runner in track as well. His 1600 times would have put him on varsity most years. He was not as strong mentally as other runners on the team though. He was very unsure of himself and was often afraid to push through pain. Dave and Devon were confident they could work with him and shape him into a competitive runner on varsity. He had the natural ability; he just needed to match that with some mental toughness.

Junior Phil Kronenberg was a dark horse candidate. He had run more days than anyone else last summer at Downers Grove South's practices and continued to work hard throughout the track season. He was excited to be doing York Camp and was very optimistic about his chances of making the varsity team. Phil lacked some of the natural ability the other runners on the team possessed though. Despite that, he was going to try his best to work harder than everyone else on the team and emerge as one of the top runners in the fall.

Sophomores Andy Mitchell and Matt Davoren were surprise additions to the squad that would be heading to York Camp. They both ran cross country and were pretty talented, but neither of them ran track. Andy was a swimmer and Matt a baseball player. They were good friends and had agreed to do this together. Devon and Dave were friends with both of them and had often talked with them about doing York Camp. They both agreed to do it. They would both be in for quite the surprise. They had barely run during the spring, and they were about to start the hardest training program in the state.

Another surprising addition to the group was sophomore Andrew Quigley. He had been near the bottom of the team in cross country and had showed almost no desire to work hard. He worked harder and began to show more interest in track. He posted some good times during the season, but Devon and Dave had not talked with him much about doing York Camp. Neither of them thought he had the desire to go through with it. To their surprise, he approached them towards the end of the track season and said he wanted to do it with everyone else.

Dave and Devon sat at a team meeting that Coach Keogh called near the beginning of summer. They looked over the group that they would be trying to make into runners capable of matching the success of the previous year's legendary team. They both knew the odds were stacked against them. No one else in the state was expecting much out of Downers Grove South this upcoming year. They were thought of as a one-and-done team that had just gotten lucky. Everyone else thought they would sink back into obscurity after losing five of their seven varsity runners. Dave and Devon were skeptical themselves. The only one of these runners that was relatively prepared and knew what he was signing up for was Steve. The year before, the top seven had already been good runners that became better. This group was a mix of good and mediocre runners that would have to come a long way in order to seriously compete in the state. They were also very inexperienced. Almost all of them were sophomores. Not one of them had ever run a varsity race in cross country. Dave and Devon certainly had their work cut out for them.

Nevertheless, Dave and Devon were sure of two things. They trusted each other to put their heart and soul into improving themselves and the rest of the team, and they were sure of the roaring fire that burned inside of each of them. Both of them still felt the pain of the loss at Sectionals just as clearly as the day that it happened. They both came into the summer knowing what to expect at York Camp and ready to work harder than they had ever worked before. The amount of effort they would put forth this summer would make last summer look like a walk in the park. Together, they were determined to make themselves, and their teammates, a force to be reckoned with for the second year in a row. If by only sheer will, they would make this group into a contender. Nothing could hold them back. They went into the first day of York Camp anxious to take their first steps towards rekindling the dream.

The Return of Kell and Kapp

In Devon's room, he heard his alarm clock go off. He didn't need it. He had been wide awake for almost half an hour. He could not wait to get out there and run at his first day back at York Camp. He had been waiting for this day for months. After a disappointing track season, he just wanted to start training for cross country. He trained through the end of track and up until the start of summer training to make sure he would be ready to start his second summer at York Camp. As he left to pick up his teammates, he could barely contain his excitement. This began his campaign to exorcise the demons from the end of last year's season. He had kept the pain from the Sectional loss close to his heart because he knew he would need it. This was going to drive him to work harder than anyone else in the state. This was going to drive him to be the best runner on the team. This was going to drive him to train another legendary team. He couldn't wait to get started.

Early on a warm and sunny June morning, the eight runners were driving up to the first day of York Camp. In Devon's car he excitedly told Andy, Steve, and Chris what to expect this summer. They were all very nervous. None of them had ever undertaken such a difficult task. Andy had missed almost five months of running in between the end of cross country and the start of outdoor track. As they listened to Devon elaborate on the workouts and mileage that they would be running, they were having doubts about whether or not this was a good idea. They admired the passion and desire that Dave and Devon had but thought it was something they didn't possess. They didn't know how they were going to survive this summer. The car pulled up to the park that they would be training in for two months. They walked over to where all the runners were meeting with no idea of what to expect.

Dave pulled up in his car with Matt, Phil, and Andrew along with him. He looked at Devon and could tell he was thinking the exact same thing. They couldn't wait to start this summer off on the right track. The team walked over to check in with Coach Joe Newton. He had remembered Devon and Dave from the year before. Mr. Newton gave everyone nicknames by shortening their last names. Dave was Kapp and Devon was Kell. Mr. Newton was glad to see them back. They both had worked very hard for him last summer, and it disappointed him to see that they didn't make it to State. He warmly greeted both of them and told them to sit down and wait with everyone else.

Mr. Newton addressed the more than two-hundred runners that had come from all over the state to run at York Camp this summer with his thought for the day. The thought for the day today was the same one from the first day last year: "Every day you make a choice to be mediocre, good, or great. If you choose to be mediocre that's all you're ever going to be." That fired up Dave and Devon even more. They wanted to make a statement today. They wanted to show everyone they were ready to come here and run step for step with the best athletes in the state.

The workout was a long distance run. Devon and Dave ran at the front from the start. Two York runners stayed with them for a little while, but by the end of the run, Dave and Devon finished in front of everyone else. Everyone was impressed. They had both been good last summer, but they came back looking like different runners. They ran with purpose and carried themselves like champions. The rest of the runners needed to get used to it. These two would be seen at the front of workouts everyday at York Camp. They had taken their first steps towards reaching their rekindled dream, and their steps had been large. The sky was the limit for Kell and Kapp.

While Dave and Devon were leading the run, the rest of the team showed promise. They were all running together. They encouraged each other and kept each other going. At the end of the run, they all had run more in this run than they ever had in a single day before. They were exhausted, but they had gotten through it. Devon and Dave were impressed. Perhaps they had something to work with. Maybe making this team into a winner would not be as hard as they had thought. As they headed home, they all dreamed of what this team could be capable of. Every single one of them had gotten off to a great start today. They would need this initial confidence boost because it would only get harder from here.

Live Your Dreams

Three weeks into York Camp, some members of the team adapted to it better than others. Steve had to closely monitor his mileage because his shins hurt constantly. His shins had been a problem towards the end of track, and now they caused him pain daily. If he wasn't careful, he would develop stress fractures and be out for the season. Many days he couldn't run at all and would have to ride his bike. Despite this setback, he continued to train hard riding his bike several hours per day and running when his shins felt better.

Phil took to the training well. He had come into the summer in shape and ready to work, and he had more than enough of that now. He completed almost every run in full and was making the other runners nervous that he would be ahead of them when the season started.

Andy, Chris, and Matt survived one day at a time. They had run more in these three weeks than they had probably run collectively in the last year. Every day when they came home, they would be terribly exhausted and sleep through most of the day. Nevertheless, they were showing improvement. They tended to run in a pack and work together to finish the run.

The big surprise so far was Andrew. No one had too great of expectations for him at the start, but he was doing better than most of the team. He completed the majority of his runs and kept up with or ran ahead of his teammates. He showed a real desire to work hard and was making a big impression on Dave and Devon.

On the other hand, Dave and Devon had no trouble getting accustomed to the intense training. They came into York Camp ready and constantly ran with the top runners from York's team. The only runners that would be seen finishing ahead of Dave and Devon would be the top two runners from York. Mr. Newton was extremely impressed with the work ethic of the Mustangs' top two runners. He would often joke with them that he would buy them houses just to move them to York to run.

The two of them took this success in stride. It became their daily expectation to lead the run. During track workouts, they would often set the pace for most of York's varsity. Dave and Devon were running even with or beating runners that had been All-State last year. Most of York's runners hadn't even heard of the two of them but here they were, ambitiously challenging their top runners every day. Many things were uncertain about Downers South's team but one thing was clear; they had two fearless leaders that were going to do everything they could to score points for the team.

Dave and Devon became more motivated with every day that passed. They both ran in the afternoon as well to supplement their morning workout. Devon continued to lift weights to make sure he could be the fittest runner in the state. Dave did plenty of upper body work as well. His successful track season made him optimistic that he could be not just the best runner on the team this year, but the best runner ever to run at Downers Grove South. They ran no less than eighty miles in a week and never cut a run short. The two of them were so even in workouts it was impossible to tell who was better. For every time that Dave would edge out Devon in a speed workout, Devon would lead a long distance run. They ran step for step with each other and worked together to make each other as good as they possibly could be every day. One of Mr. Newton's thoughts for the day that really stuck with them was; "live your dreams; if anyone tries to say you can't then screw 'em." Devon and Dave were living their dreams right now. They were running with the best runners in the state and getting ready to become names that their competition would learn to respect. They were going to be a force that other teams would have to plan for. They were going to make it impossible for what had happened last year to happen again.

This Team is Different

For all the energy Dave and Devon expended trying to keep their teammates motivated and on task, one thing was very different about this team than the previous year's team; they had no problems getting along. One of the miracles of last year's squad was how everyone was able to put their egos aside and come together. This group was very close from the start. Many of them were already friends, and they were much more interested in running with each other instead of against each other. They never had any heated arguments or bragged about who was faster. They were in this together and needed each other to get through this rigorous training program.

It helped immensely that all eight of them trained together. Every day when they drove up to York Camp, they would always talk and get to know each other better. On the way home, they would excitedly boast about how much they were improving and how excited they were about the season. No one had to put their egos aside because they were all interested in seeing each other succeed. This great camaraderie was a direct result of the great leadership from their captains.

Devon and Dave worked just as hard to help their teammates out as they did to help themselves improve. They wanted this team to be a real team from the start. They wanted them to embrace each other as brothers and rely on each other when they were tired and scared. They referred their teammates to their great physical therapist, Dr. Mike, whenever someone injured themselves. They would invite the team over to their house to hang out after practice and on the weekends. Right away there was a great chemistry between all of them.

The team really came together when they all went to running camp at University of Wisconsin for the second summer in a row. They would all sneak out of activities during the day, go swimming at night, and always found something fun to do together. The whole week was so much fun for them that they didn't want to see it end. Another thing that happened at Wisconsin Camp was the state took notice of two new competitors emerging on the scene.

Many other very talented runners attended camp at University of Wisconsin and on the first day there was a race to separate all the runners into training groups. Dave and Devon made quite the statement in the race. Devon finished in the top ten and Dave was not far behind him. The other runners wondered who these new stand-outs were. After the week was over, the team went home with their two leaders having emerged as forces to be reckoned with in the state and a team that had never been closer. This rebuilding project looked like it might just work out.

Two Horses

At the end of the summer, just as the official practices were beginning, Coach Keogh wanted to see just what he had to work with. He needed to see how fit his runners were and who his top athletes were. He scheduled a two mile time trial for the Saturday two weeks before their first meet at Lyons Township. This was a welcome relief for many of the runners because, after a long summer of hard work, they wanted to see just how good they were. They had talked often in practice about how they couldn't wait to see how much this training had paid off for them. The team gathered on a warm and sunny Saturday morning in mid-August, anxious to get out and stretch their legs.

They put their spikes on, warmed up, and gathered on the line. The entire team would be running so everyone was elbow-to-elbow with the person next to them. Dave and Devon had felt great warming up. They felt fast. Both of them looked at each other as they stepped up to the line ready to show everyone just how good they were. They didn't disappoint.

Bang!

Coach Keogh fired the gun and the runners were off. Immediately, Dave and Devon pulled away from everyone else. At the mile no one else was even close to them. Coach Keogh and Coach Bicicchi couldn't believe what they saw. Dave and Devon didn't even look like they were trying. They ran together just as smoothly and on pace as if they were going on an easy afternoon jog. They approached the final lap dead even. Just as it had been all summer, it was impossible to distinguish who was better. Each was just as fast and just as determined as the other. They cruised to a final time of 9:53; forty seconds ahead of the next finisher. It didn't even look they were breathing hard afterward. They gave each other an excited high five. The coaches knew they had two studs on their hands. They were fit. They were focused. They were ready.

The rest of the team performed pretty well overall. Steve, Chris, Andy, Andrew, and Matt were the next finishers behind Dave and Devon. Their times were promising, but it was clear they still needed to do a lot of work. Finishing not far behind them were two surprises. Sophomore Craig Schieve, who had been a standout on the team as a freshman, was not far behind the top seven runners. He trained with the rest of the team at Downers South over the summer and looked like he might have a chance at running varsity. Behind Craig was first year runner Sunil Bean. He had not run in his entire life before this and had decided to try it out this year as a junior. He ran a very impressive time for having so little experience. Phil finished not far behind Sunil. At the end of the time trial, Coach Keogh and Bicicchi were encouraged by what they had seen. It looked like they might have another good team this year. Their chances looked great with their two horses leading the way.

After the time trial was over everyone went over to have breakfast afterwards. Devon stayed behind a little while longer to stretch. He had tweaked his groin muscle a few days earlier, and he really felt it now. It had worried him going into the race but felt fine while he was warming up. He must have aggravated it while he was running. Devon stretched it out, got some ice, and didn't think anything of it for the rest of the weekend. On Monday, they ran their usual workout on the track. During warm-ups, Devon knew something was wrong. The bad thing about a groin injury is it barely feels like anything until it is seriously hurt. Devon gutted out twelve quarter mile repeats but couldn't do anymore. His groin was killing him. That was the last time he would be able to work out or race for almost two weeks. Despite doing heavy doses of daily stretching and physical therapy it would not heal fast enough. A groin injury takes time to heal no matter what one does for it. This would be something that he would be dealing with for the rest of the season.

The Team opens up the season Short-Handed

Going into the first meet of the season at the Lyons Township Invitational, the Mustangs would be fielding a depleted team. Devon had run very sparingly over the last two weeks due to his groin injury and would not be running today. Andy had experienced some pain in his hip for the last week and decided at the last minute to sit the race out. Down two of their best runners, the team headed out ready to race anyway. Coach Keogh and Bicicchi spoke with their runners and left them at the line. Then, they did something new which they would do at every meet this season; Dave and Devon, the captains, gave their teammates their own pre-race motivational speech. This meant a lot to the rest of the team hearing these words of encouragement from their teammates. After they broke out of the team huddle, Devon and Andy ran off to watch from the sidelines.

The entire varsity team, besides Dave, had never run a varsity race before. They were very nervous. Steve put a lot of pressure on himself and wanted to match his success from track. His shins were doing much better than they had been earlier in the summer, and he felt tense but ready to race. Chris, Matt, and Andrew were all very unsure of what to expect from themselves. They had been working hard but were worried because they were fatigued from all of the miles they had been putting in. Devon and Dave told them they were supposed to feel that way, but nevertheless, they wanted to be able to do their best and race well. There would be a lot more competition on varsity their year. As opposed to last season, when the top seven were far and above everyone else, only Dave and Devon's spots were assured. Craig and Sunil had not finished far behind the top seven in the time trial and would be getting one of their spots if they did not perform well.

Bang!

The race started. Dave headed out with the lead runners. Dave was an aggressive runner that was not afraid to go out hard to challenge the top runners in the race. At the mile, he was in the lead. Further back, Steve looked good early on. He had gotten out to a strong first mile and was near twentieth place. About twenty seconds behind him, Chris was doing well in his first performance on varsity. There were large expectations for him which he was not comfortable with. He was not as competitive or aggressive as some of the other guys on the team and often felt intimidated by them. Despite his fears, he ran strong and was only ten places behind Steve. Matt tried to keep pace with Chris. Similar to Chris, Matt feared for his spot on varsity. He had worked hard for it and didn't want to lose it after the first race. Chris pulled away from him as the race went on, but Matt still managed to maintain a good pace. About twenty seconds behind Matt was Andrew. Andrew felt more tired than the rest of the team, and it showed. He looked very lethargic, and it was evident that he was struggling throughout the entire race.

Coming into the final mile Dave still looked great. He tucked in firmly with a pack of five runners at the front of the race ready to give it all he had. One runner had pulled away early on and these five had stuck together the entire race since then. Another runner broke away from the pack, and it didn't look like anyone would be catching up with him. It was between Dave and three other competitors to see who would get second place. Dave was running alongside a collection of All-State runners. None of them recognized him, but he would make them remember his name today. He ran out ahead of the pack and was in third place with a half mile to go. The four runners battled and took turns leading the pack. It came down to the final quarter mile. It was an all out sprint from here. Dave put his head down and went for it. He was digging hard but couldn't catch up to two of the runners who started to pull away. He edged out another runner as they crossed the line to finish in fifth place. His time was fifty seconds faster than what he had run on this course last year. All of the other runners wondered who this was in the dark blue jersey that had just come out of nowhere to take fifth place in a very fast race. Dave would be taking many other runners by surprise this season. He had arrived and was not going anywhere.

Almost a minute behind Dave, Steve made his move to begin his kick. He used his great natural speed and passed up several runners in the last mile to come across the line in twenty-third place. He had improved his time considerably from last year's race. Although he wouldn't admit it, he had done very well to start the season off. Chris finished thirty seconds behind Steve. He fell back during the race when he began feeling pain in his groin. It had noticeably slowed him as the race went on. He would not race again for a month. Matt finished about fifteen seconds behind Chris. He had performed decently for his first varsity race, but he would need to put in a lot of work if he expected to stay on the varsity team. Andrew had run the entire race tired, and his time reflected that. He was almost thirty seconds behind Matt. The surprise of the day came out of the junior varsity race. Sunil had taken third place with a time that would have put him at fourth on the varsity team. He had some serious talent and was officially part of the varsity team after this race.

After their first race, the Mustangs had made no serious statements. They looked like they would live up to their low pre-season expectations. The team showed promise but still had a long way to go. They were injured and inexperienced. They headed into next week's race with many uncertainties. Would Devon be able to run? Would they be able to replace Chris? Were the first time varsity runners ready to compete on the big stage? Coach Keogh, Coach Bicicchi, Dave, and Devon all had a lot to occupy their minds. This team was going to require a lot of work.

Racing at the Promised Land

There were three races held at Detweiller Park in Peoria throughout the season, and these meets brought out many teams anxious to run on the State Meet course. A meet at Peoria was a preview of what the State Meet would be like. Out of the three invitationals held at Detweiller Park throughout the regular season, the first one was the most competitive. It brought out forty-seven teams from around the state. The top three schools attending were contenders to be top five in the state. Dave and Devon had been getting after Coach Keogh all summer to enter the team into this meet. It was held the same weekend as the Marmion Invitational which was not a very competitive meet. The two captains desperately wanted to make it into the Peoria Invite. It would be the best competition they would face until the State Series and allow them to run some great times on Peoria's fast course.

On the Monday before the race, Coach Keogh announced at practice they had been accepted to run there. This excited the team very much. They wanted a chance to run a great race as a team. Devon and Andy had been cleared to run, and Sunil was being moved up to varsity so they would be fielding a full seven man varsity team. These three additions would make up for the loss of Chris as well. After a hard week of practice, the team left school early on Friday to make the three hour trip down to Peoria. Their spirits soared the entire way down. They blasted music and joked amongst themselves. All of them were excited to run a great race tomorrow.

They arrived at the course and did an easy run to get the accustomed to the conditions they would be running in tomorrow. Only Dave and Devon had run here before and that was only in a workout. It was important that they all had an idea of what to expect. The team brimmed with enthusiasm as they jogged the course. It was a beautiful day, and they all imagined coming back here for the State Meet in two months. They ran some sprints and then climbed back into the van to check into their hotel.

That night, the team kept their moods light as they went out to dinner and came back to the hotel for the night. They weren't even worried about the race. They were just a group of friends having a good time at a hotel for the weekend. Things couldn't have been better.

After Dave and Devon retired to their room for the night, the rest of the team stayed up late joking around with each other and playing pranks on Dave and Devon. This team could have easily been mistaken for a group of kids just down to party for a weekend. They were a wild bunch that seemed to never take anything seriously. This is what made this team so close. No one felt as if another was above them. They were just a group of friends that liked to enjoy themselves but knew when it was time to get down business.

In his room, Devon worried about his injury. He had been icing it all night and was having a lot of anxiety about his race tomorrow. He knew his groin was not completely healthy. If he pushed himself when his muscle wasn't ready to deal with the strain, he could make the injury considerably worse. His worries kept him up until late in the night. On the other side of the room, Dave lay in bed awake for different reasons. He was filled with confidence from last week's race and couldn't wait to get out there tomorrow. This was his chance to really arrive on the scene as a great runner in the state. The eyes of the entire state would be focused on this race tomorrow, and he wanted to put on a big performance.

They woke up early the next morning and went to eat breakfast with the coaches. They met in Coach Keogh's room and, after a short talk about the race; they got into the van and headed to the course. On the ride over everyone was very serious. It was time to get down to business. They all listened to their iPods and thought about the race ahead. Dave felt great and ready to dominate today. Devon was unsure how his injury would hold up. Steve recognized how big the stage that he would be running on today was and prepared himself mentally for the race ahead. Andy was uncertain of what to expect out of his first varsity race but felt excited to prove he belonged here. Andrew wanted to show his teammates he was better than what they had seen from him last week. He knew his spot on varsity was hanging in the balance. Matt was not in a good place mentally. He and his girlfriend had broken up the night before and that was occupying his thoughts rather than the race. Sunil didn't know what to expect. This was only his second cross country race ever, and he was expected to come out here and perform on the varsity team at this huge race. They pulled into Detweiller Park, Coach Keogh parked the van, and they walked out into the bright morning sun. They looked at the roughly thousand people that lined the course. The seven of them couldn't wait to put on a great show for all these spectators.

Someone who they were all glad to see back was Joe. He had joined them last week at Lyons Township and was documenting their season. Joe had gotten into filming after his season-ending injury in the spring. No one had seen much of him since he had gotten hurt and all those that knew him were happy to see him back. Having Joe around relieved Dave and Devon because Joe had always been someone they looked up to. It was good to have someone they could depend on for help when everyone else always looked to them for guidance. Joe joked around with his two good friends and helped them relax before the race.

Twenty minutes before the race started Coach Keogh and Coach Bicicchi assembled their runners. They had them do some practice starts, gave them their pre-race pep talk, and left them at the line. Once again the seven of them had the captain-led team huddle after the coaches left. Dave and Devon made it clear and simple. This was a big stage with great competition so they better go out and give all these people a good show.

As they took their place on the line they looked down the line at all the other racers. There were three hundred and twenty-six other runners. It just began to set in on them how massive this event really was. The starter gave the final commands over a megaphone. The thousands of runners and spectators all went quiet. As Joe filmed the team from the sidelines, he focused in on Dave and Devon. The look on both their faces was one of total concentration and readiness.

Bang!

The gun fired and three hundred and twenty-six runners took off. There were so many people all running close together it sounded like a stampede of buffalo. Out in the front of the race, Evan Jager, who was the top runner in the state and had a chance of beating the state record for an individual performance at Detweiller Park, took the lead. Behind him, the leaders formed into a pack. As the mob of runners began to separate out, Dave moved his way towards the front. He was on his way to having a great race.

Immediately from the gun, Devon could tell he was not running at one hundred percent. He had worked out once in the last three weeks, and his mileage was but a fraction of what it had been before he had gotten hurt. It didn't help that this was an especially hot and humid day. The runners had been sweating just standing at the starting line. A mile into the race, Devon felt terrible and knew this was going to be a long race. Steve noticed Devon was going out slow so he decided to stick with him for as long as he could. Steve did not feel great either. He had been working very hard in practice, and his legs felt even more fatigued in this humidity. As he crossed the mile, not far behind Devon, he could already tell he was slowing down. This would not be easy for him either.

Andy and Sunil on the other hand both felt great. They were off and running with authority today. They had established a strong pace early on and worked off of each other to progressively move up in the race. Behind them, Andrew was doing better than last week but was still in some trouble. He still felt fatigued and sluggish from all the work he had been putting in. For the second week in a row, it would be an uphill battle for him throughout race. Matt was in some serious trouble. Less than two hundred meters into the race, he had twisted his ankle in a hole in the ground. This had strained a muscle in his lower leg, and he was in a lot of pain. He would have to limp through the entire race.

The coaches were very excited. Dave was running in great position at the front of the race. He was in contention to be in the top ten. In the last mile, Dave finished with a great kick. He approached the last quarter mile, which was a long straightaway until the finish.

Using his mile-runner speed, he put a move on a group that he had been running with and sped ahead of them. He ran the last two hundred meters in a dead sprint. Overcoming the heat and ignoring his tired legs, he ran to a ninth place finish. He was overjoyed. This was an incredible performance. There would be no denying after today that Dave had arrived on the scene as a legitimate candidate to be an All-State runner.

Devon had been fighting his own fatigue the entire race and when it was down to the final quarter mile, he felt like he had nothing left. He gave his best effort and managed to cross the line twenty-five seconds behind Dave. This was not how he had pictured starting off his season. As he waited for his teammates to finish, he knew that it would take a lot longer than he wanted to believe to get himself healthy and back in shape.

Steve had been warming up as the race went on and was in good position going through the last mile. He put on a speed burst on the final quarter-mile straightaway and crossed the line eight seconds faster than he run had last week. He was in good shape for his second race of the season. As always, he was hard on himself, but his coaches and his teammates could tell that he was returning to form. To everyone's delight the fourth and fifth runners, Andy and Sunil, did great. They finished not far behind Steve. Andy had opened up his season with a statement race. Sunil came out of nowhere to run times that most runners had to train for years to run. This surprise runner would be a huge asset to this team.

Andrew struggled through his race and crossed the line faster than last week but still not as fast as he needed to be. He still had his spot on varsity, but he knew if he wanted to keep it for long, he was going to need to start performing better. Matt hobbled in a minute behind Andrew. There was obviously something wrong. He told everyone about how he had gotten his foot caught and fallen down at the start of the race. He would courageously continue to run in practice, but this injury would be working against him for the rest of the season.

Heading back home the team had more to be encouraged about after this race. Their top runner was a stud and everyone knew once Devon was back in shape, he would be right behind Dave. Steve was coming along as a very strong third runner. Their fourth and fifth runners had emerged as great assets to the team. The team still had health issues as well as many uncertainties but one day at a time, it would continue to improve. Getting on the bus to go home, Devon had made a bold statement; "remember this course, because we'll be back here in two months." They prayed he was right.

Protect This House

The Monday after the Peoria Invite, the Mustangs easily won a dual meet against a weak Conference team. They trained right through the race, running several miles before, purposefully holding back during, and running more miles after the race was over. The coaches were planning ahead for the Mustang Invite at O'Brien Park coming up on Saturday. The team had narrowly missed out on winning the year before and wanted to come back and put on a winning performance this year. Coach Bicicchi was already planning out his motivational speech that he would give before the race on Monday. He wanted to make sure his runners would be ready to go out and do their job this weekend.

The team stuck to the workout schedule and continued to train hard throughout the week. This intense training schedule was taking its toll on almost everyone. Very few members of the team were not injured. Devon had come up with the workout schedule himself, and it seemed as if his ambition blinded his better judgment. They had only one slow-paced recovery run during the week, and some weeks didn't have any at all. Devon hadn't considered that the rest of the team, besides Dave, were not physically or mentally ready to handle such a strenuous schedule. They had only done this kind of training for one summer. Devon and Dave had been doing this for a year. Even Devon wasn't making it through this schedule unscathed. His groin injury still required at least one hour of physical therapy and stretching everyday just to keep it from getting worse. The coaches were worried about their runners. Someone had gotten hurt in every race so far. For now, their focus was on preparing the team for Saturday's home invite.

For the second year in a row, a large crowd gathered at O'Brien Park. The team had done much work to create hype for the race, and once again it had paid off. Spectators lined the course by the start of the first race of the day. At the Downers Grove South camp, the runners were calm. They were optimistic about their chances this year. The team had showed a lot of potential last week at Peoria, and they hoped to ride that momentum into this race. All of a sudden, they noticed many of the varsity runners for the other contender to win today, Saint Charles North, were running hours before the varsity race. They thought they were just going to field a subpar team and still win this race. This was an insult to the Mustangs. They were not going to be a doormat that Saint Charles could just walk over. This was their home course, and they were going to show this team just how good they were.

The team began their warm-up jog. It was close to noon, and for the second week in a row the weather was very humid and muggy. To make the conditions even worse, it had rained all week so the course was muddy. The captains could sense their teammates were nervous so they did what they could to make everyone laugh and lighten the mood. The team stretched out, did their practice starts, and huddled together for the pre-race motivational speech. Coach Bicicchi knelt down in the middle of the huddle. He looked each one of his athletes in the eye, and then he started to get fired up. He stressed that they needed to go out and establish that they were the better team right away. They could not let this subpar varsity team that Saint Charles was fielding get any hope that they might have a chance at winning. He said his two leaders needed to get out in front, and the rest of the team needed to follow their lead. All of a sudden, someone butted in.

Devon had been especially insulted by Saint Charles overlooking his team. His teammates were his brothers, and it was a personal insult for them to be slapped in the face like this. The blatant lack of respect they were being shown was unacceptable. He kept this in mind going into the pre-race huddle. Usually, when he and Dave addressed the team before the race they would wait until after the coaches had spoken to them. They would not try to get too intense. The main thing they wanted to accomplish was to give a few encouraging words and go over the race strategy one last time. Today called for something more. This was their home course. This was their house. Devon did not want to be disrespected in front of their home fans.

In the middle of Coach Bicicchi's speech, Devon decided to cut in. He passionately addressed his brothers; "these guys think they can come out here and field some team of scrubs and still win. They think we're just some team they can blow off and roll right over. Well we're better than that. This is our house and we must protect it. We're going to go out and show them that we are still a team to be reckoned with. We are just as dangerous as we were a year ago and today is the day the state realizes this. We will go out there, and we will protect this house!"

Coach Bicicchi and Dave had nothing to add. They all had heard enough. Exhilarated by their captain's fiery speech, they were ready to put on a show for the home fans. They broke out the huddle on "our house!" and jogged up to the line. Devon went to each one of his teammates in the waning seconds before the race to give them one last piece of motivation. They stepped to the line, listened to the starter's commands, and…

Bang!

The race was off. Dave did not need any extra motivation for this race. He had woken up feeling great and ready to run. He was ready to start the race the moment he had arrived at the course. The four hour wait until the race started was excruciatingly long but here it finally was. Dave rode in on a wave of confidence after he had emerged as an All-State caliber runner this season. This was his home course, and he wanted to put on a great performance for the home fans. Ten seconds after the gun went off, the race for first place was over. Dave went out in a dead sprint and didn't look back. He knew there was no one else in this race that could run with him today. A quarter-mile into the race, he had a ten second lead over the second place runner. At the mile, he was twenty seconds ahead and in complete control. If the course hadn't been so muddy and the weather so humid he might have made a run at the course record. He was unstoppable today. After he was half-way through the race, he slowed down because he was so far ahead. He cruised past the line, easily winning by ten seconds. Reporters from the local papers were all over him after the race. All of the home fans poured over him; congratulating him on his stellar performance. They couldn't believe how well he had done. From start to finish, he was in total control of the race. As he watched his teammates finish, Dave felt certain that he was going to State this year. Nothing could stop him. He was on top of the world. The day was his, and no one could take it away from him.

As Dave was putting first place away, the rest of the race unfolded behind him. Devon had tried to go out with Dave, but he was just going too damn fast. Throughout the first mile, he kept pace with the top runner from Saint Charles. They battled back and forth, each trying to leave the other behind. Devon was still wary of his injury and hesitant to push it too far. Then, coming up on the two-mile marker, one of his friends got after him. His friend was a runner himself and knew how hard Devon had worked to get to this point. He didn't want to see Devon let his fear hold him back. He ran next to Devon for a few meters reminding him of all the miles he had run and all the pain he had gone through. What was it all for if he wasn't going to put it to use and leave this other guy behind? This was exactly what Devon needed to hear. He put his fear behind him and rapidly quickened his pace. Coming up to a large hill, Devon knew this was his chance to put this guy behind him for good. There might be faster runners but there were few stronger than Devon. He used hills as an advantage over other runners. Hills would break some competitors at this point of a race. Devon used this hill to break his competitor. Putting his head down, he barreled up the hill and then sprinted down the other side. By the time he had gotten to the bottom, the other runner was well behind him. Devon kept his pace up and finished the race in second. Downers South was off to a great start.

Despite the humidity and mud, Steve felt great. He had been keeping pace with a pack of three runners until he made a move half-way through the race and left them in his dust. He progressively sped up over the last mile and was alone in fifth place throughout the rest of the race. He crossed the line having run his best race thus far. His shins bothered him, but he fought through it and finished with his best time ever at O'Brien Park's course. The Mustangs had three out of the first five finishers. The race was all but over.

Andy was having another strong race. He had caught up to the pack of runners Steve had left behind and stuck with them for the whole race. The humidity bothered him, but he just put it out of his mind and kept going. Coming into the final half-mile, he was running with two other athletes. He tried to kick but something held him back. His hip injury that had held him out of the first race of the year started acting up. Andy crossed the line with a great time but with definite pain in his hip. This would be a serious detriment to the Mustangs in the very near future.

Sunil performed great in his second varsity race. He tried keeping pace with Andy but was unable to cope with the adverse conditions and fell behind. Sunil's inexperience was working against him. He was not used to dealing with pain in a race. This was only the fourth race he had ever run in his life. Despite his struggles, he crossed the line with a phenomenal time. He was the last scoring runner for Downers South at twelfth place. The race was over. The Mustangs had sealed their victory.

Andrew and Matt's difficulties continued. Andrew once again did not feel strong going into this race. The humidity and mud were too much for him, and he had a disappointing race for the third week in a row. Matt's sprained tendon in his lower leg was too painful to bear. He limped from the start. His time was a miracle considering the pain he endured throughout race. Once again, Downers South had multiple runners pulling up lame at the end of a race.

Despite the injuries they sustained, the Mustangs had reemerged as a contender in the state. They recorded the best team score ever in the Mustang Invite. Saint Charles' disrespect of the team had only given them the extra motivation they needed to put on a great performance. This was their best team performance all year. The coaches beamed over their runners as they watched the awards ceremony. They were more excited than they had been all year. Not only did they have another great team on their hands but they had two exceptional captains to lead the way. This was all very encouraging heading into the dual meet against Conference rival Hinsdale South. Unfortunately for the Mustangs, the Conference would not be so easy to take this year.

The Conference is Lost

As usual, the dual meet against Hinsdale South was held the Monday following the Mustang Invite. Last year had been a near disaster, with the Mustangs barely beating Hinsdale South's team. This year, Devon and Dave made certain they would not be caught off guard. Whoever won this meet would be guaranteed at least a share of the Conference Title. The captains had been stressing since the summer to focus on beating their Conference rival. This year, they were a much more formidable team. Their two standout sophomores from the year before had developed into elite runners. They had a young but talented team, similar to the Mustangs. Heading into the race, it was hard to tell which team would have the advantage. Both teams had talent, but injuries hindered their success. Hinsdale's best runner from a year ago, Alex Wright, had missed several months with a mysterious back issue, and was a long way from being the near-State Qualifier he was a year before. For the Mustangs, Devon was still recovering, Andy was not sure if he would be able to run, and Chris and Matt would both be watching the race from the sidelines. To make things even worse, it was an extremely windy day and the course they were running on was wide open with nothing to block the wind. Both teams knew this would be a battle.

Dave and Devon addressed the team before the race and made sure they were ready for a fight to the finish. No one could underestimate this team because after being blown out at the Conference meet the year before, they were looking for revenge this year. The coaches wasted no time in starting the race. Soon after arriving at the course, both teams were lined up and ready to run.

Bang!

The gun went off, and the race to take the lead in the West Suburban Gold Conference was on. Once again, Dave ran out in front. He was determined to win this race. He wanted to be the best runner in the Conference, and this was his chance to show Hinsdale's top runners just how good he was. One of Hinsdale's top two runners, Brian Denk, went with him. As the two of them left the rest of the race behind, Devon fought to keep pace with Hinsdale's other top runner, Lee Vlcek. He barely made it to the mile before Vlcek left him behind. Not only was Devon feeling discomfort in his groin but he was especially vulnerable against the wind. No matter how hard he tried to fight through it, the powerful gusts just kept slowing him down. With a mile left in the race, Devon knew he had no chance to catch up to Vlcek.

The rest of the Downers South team was having just as much trouble as Devon. This team was a collection of skinnier guys that didn't have a lot of upper body strength to push through conditions such as these. Steve tried to keep pace with Hinsdale's third and fourth runners, but it was to no avail. They just kept putting more ground between him and themselves until they had pulled away for good. Sunil was trying to keep pace with Hinsdale's fifth runner, but he was fighting a losing battle as well. Even if he beat their fifth runner, Hinsdale already had a commanding lead. As the coaches watched from the sideline, they knew half-way through the race that it was over. Dave won the race, but that would be the only bright spot for the Mustangs. Devon finished in fourth place, twenty seconds behind Hinsdale's second runner. Steve was beaten by their third and fourth runners, and their fifth runner beat out Sunil by five seconds in the end. Finishing after Sunil, and well out of the position of making any difference, was sophomore Craig Schieve, Andrew, and Andy hobbled across as the last varsity runner for the Mustangs. They had no other varsity runners to put in the race. The other two were hurt. Coach Keogh and Coach Bicicchi gathered their disheartened team and boarded the bus back to school. It would be a long ride. The coaches knew something needed to be changed.

Making Necessary Changes

The next day at practice, Coach Keogh had a long talk with his varsity team. First of all, the workout schedule needed to be changed. It was just too much for them to handle. Too many runners were getting hurt instead of getting benefits from this. Secondly, Craig Schieve would now be practicing with the varsity. He had finished with the sixth best time on the team running the sophomore race at the Mustang Invite and finished fifth on the team against Hinsdale. He was a talented runner that they needed to have if they wanted to be the best team they could be. Devon was outraged. He did not see the logic in this. His single-minded obsession with reaching his dreams was not allowing him to understand why these changes were being made. He wanted to run his workout schedule that he had drawn up no matter what sacrifices needed to be made. He also didn't accept this newcomer to the varsity squad. In his mind, he had gone through so much with his teammates over the summer, and he wanted to make it all the way through with them and them only. Coach Keogh wrapped up his speech, and the team set out on a much needed recovery run.

The team and the coaches did not appreciate Devon's bitter attitude. They all knew this was the right decision and didn't understand why he wasn't accepting it. Devon, Steve, and Andrew fell behind the others and snuck off to do their own workout. The scheduled workout for the day had been half-mile repeats and that was what they did. They were angry and wanted to start making sure that they would not just bow down to Hinsdale the next time they met at the Conference Meet. Running through fatigue, pain, and an unseasonably cold, blustery day, the three of them fought through the workout and headed back to school. Coach Bicicchi noticed the three coming back much later than everyone else, and he knew that Devon had most likely led the way. He took Devon aside and told him to come over to his house for a talk tonight. Coach Bicicchi needed to straighten out his captain and put him in his place.

Devon came over to Coach Bicicchi's house that night. His coach took him into his office, shut the door, and addressed him very frankly: "Devon, you're the captain and I respect you very much but you need to get your ass in line!" This hit Devon hard. His coach had never talked to him this bluntly before. Coach Bicicchi told him he needed to respect the decisions of his coaches and accept Craig as a member of the varsity whether he liked it or not. Coach Bicicchi continued on, "this workout schedule is too much…we won't even have a team left to field by the time the State Series starts up".

Devon listened to every word his coach told him. He had the utmost respect for Coach Bicicchi. If it weren't for him, Devon would not be where he was right now. With fire in his eyes and passion in his voice, Devon explained to his coach what was fueling his obsessive ambition. He explained that last year's team had performed so poorly at Sectionals because they just weren't ready. They had tapered down their training too early, which is why they had run so well at Regionals but failed to repeat the performance the next week. He explained how that pain of defeat had been driving him ever since to avenge that loss. He looked his coach squarely in the eyes and said; "Nothing is going to hold me back from bringing this team to State this year. I will not accept anything less than the best from them. They have worked so hard, and I won't let them fall short of their dreams because they are not prepared when the time comes."

Coach Bicicchi was almost taken aback by how intense Devon's words had been. He knew the fire that burnt inside him, and he knew the fervent desire that drove him. Together, they worked out a new workout plan. They both agreed on continuing to push the team as hard as they could, but they all needed some more rest. After talking for many hours, they finally parted ways for the night. Devon left with an even stronger resolve. He was going to put his pride behind him for his teammates. His ambition had blinded him to what was really best for all of them. If he really wanted to help his teammates, he first needed to get himself healthy and back in the shape he had been in at the end of summer. He swore to himself this team was going to State no matter what. He and Dave were going to lead them to the Promised Land. They would succeed where they had fallen short last year. They could not fail.

The Team Keeps Improving

Despite losing to Hinsdale South, the Mustangs were ranked for the first time all season. Their performance at the Mustang Invite had been enough to have them barely crack the top twenty-five teams in the state. The team that was ranked directly in front of them was Hinsdale South. As the team entered a two week period without a significant race, they were able to focus on their training again. During every mile of their workouts, they thought of one thing and one thing only; coming back and beating Hinsdale at the Conference Meet.

A week after the Hinsdale South dual meet was another dual meet against Conference foe Morton High School. The team did not taper back their training at all, but the coaches stressed the importance of performing well at this meet. With Craig Schieve entering the picture, as well as Matt and Chris being cleared to run again, there would be fierce competition for the top seven varsity spots. The only runners with assured spots were Dave, Devon, and Steve. Before the race, Coach Bicicchi had an idea for how to fire up his team for this low-key, Monday afternoon race. He wanted to get the point across that no one's spot was safe. His idea was to have a pretend argument with Devon but not let anyone else know about it. The team could not get the thought in their heads that anyone was above anyone else. After Devon warmed up, Coach Bicicchi took him aside and told him the plan.

The runners stretched, did their practice starts, and huddled up to listen to the pre-race talk from Coach Bicicchi. As he began to speak about what they had to do in this race Devon interrupted him; "we know coach." "What makes you think you're so special Kelly?" he shot back. "Whose job is it to speak to the team right now, yours or mine?" "Yours coach," Devon responded. His coach challenged him, "well then what are you going to do today to show me you do know what I'm talking about?" Devon boldly answered, "I'm going to run 'til I drop!" The coach turned back to the rest of the team, "are the rest of you going to run until you drop?" They all responded in unison, "yeah!" Coach Bicicchi had them all focused now. He brought them all in, "Mustangs on three; one, two, three, Mustangs!" They were fired up after that speech. The varsity team stepped to the line ready to bring the hammer down on this weaker Morton team.

Bang!

The sound of the gun gave them an extra jolt of energy, and they were off. Devon desperately wanted to win this race and show everyone he was just as good as Dave. He started out at a torrid pace with Dave following closely behind him. The conditions on this day were the best they had seen all year. It was a cool and crisp sixty-four degrees, compared to the warm and humid weather they had seen thus far. They were all feeling great and ready to put forth a good effort.

Coming through the mile, Devon and Dave had started off at a very fast pace. Both of them hit 4:50 for the mile. At this point, Dave showed that he was still in better shape than Devon and made a surge that Devon could not answer to. Dave took the lead and didn't look back. Coming through the two-mile marker, Dave looked back and saw he was well ahead. He continued to press on and finished with a time that was ten seconds faster than his remarkable Mustang Invite time. His time was good for one of the top times ever run at O'Brien Park. Once again, Dave was the first finisher on the team and looking spectacular while doing it. Devon crossed the line ten seconds after Dave. His time was his best ever, but he was still disappointed. He wanted to be up at the front with Dave and not trailing him the entire race. Devon was happy for his friend but frustrated with his own lack of improvement.

Steve had run all by himself the entire race as well. He came in fourteen seconds behind Devon with his best time ever. The team's top three looked more formidable each time they raced. Through the first three finishers, the Mustangs were as good as anyone in the state. Their fourth finisher was a surprise today. Craig had battled it out with Morton's top runner the entire race and just barely lost out to him. His time was thirty seconds faster than he had run just a little more than a week ago at the Mustang Invite. He cemented himself as a permanent member of the varsity team with this eye-opening performance. Another surprise for the day was Andrew. He finally broke out of the funk he had been in with a very strong performance, coming across as the team's fifth runner. His time was almost a minute better than it had been at the Mustang Invite. The change in the workout plan had benefitted him greatly with some much needed rest and recovery. It relieved him to finally show his teammates he deserved to be on varsity. Nipping at Andrew's heals was Andy. Andy's injury was not a factor today, and he finished with another impressive performance for the Mustangs. Not far behind Andy was Sunil, posting another solid performance. Everyone was happy to see the next two finishers for Downers South. Matt and Chris had both gotten over their injuries and were running again. For their first race back, they both looked strong, and it seemed as if things were looking up for the Mustangs. They fielded an entirely healthy varsity team for the first time all year with nine athletes capable of making the varsity team.

There were still questions that needed to be answered, but they finally looked like they might have some resolution. Devon was the healthiest he had been all year and was returning to form. Steve improved every week and made the team very dangerous with three runners that looked capable of being State Qualifiers. The rest of the team was very competitive and were pushing each other to see who would be the best each week. The addition of Craig Schieve only pushed them to try harder in practice every day. Coach Keogh and Coach Bicicchi radiated with pride as they watched their team coming together. They were moving up in the state rankings each time they raced, and it looked as if they could come back and beat Hinsdale at Conference. There was still much work to be done but plenty to look forward to.

They're not that fast…Are they?

The team suffered through two more tough weeks of practice. The weather took a turn for the worst, with several cold and windy days which didn't make running six miles of intervals on the track any easier. The coaches and the captains continued to crack the whip on their team, and each day they looked a little better. Their ailments were healing, and their confidence was growing. A week after Morton, Dave, Devon, and Steve helped pace the rest of the varsity against a Conference basement-dweller with encouraging results. They were all coming along and looking good heading into the upcoming Saturday's West Aurora Blackhawk Stampede.

After another hard week of practice, the Mustangs boarded the team bus to head up to the West Aurora Invite. The weather had been miserable all week, but today was a picturesque autumn day. The air was cool and crisp. The sun was just warm enough to make the temperature comfortable by race time. These were perfect conditions to run. As the varsity team warmed up, they felt more excited to race than they had been all year. They knew their team was good and couldn't wait to show this very competitive meet how far they had come. Dave knew there were some great runners in this race. He hadn't faced competition this good since the second week of the season, and he came in still riding a wave of confidence. Dave had put forth one dominating performance after another, and today was his day to really shine against all this great talent.

Devon was fuming with anger and frustration. He had a rough week of practice and had heard one too many questions about why he wasn't performing as well as expected this season. After giving an obscenity-laden speech to his team, he fiercely sized up his competition. He was annoyed by one team's fans who kept sounding an obnoxious horn. This only fueled the fire. Devon was barely even thinking about his race strategy. All he thought of was his anger and how he couldn't wait to unleash it on these unsuspecting runners. The captains lined up with the rest of their teammates.

Bang!

This massive race started and quickly funneled into a forest preserve about a quarter-mile after the start. Dave and a group of four others sprinted to the front of the race. Devon and Steve tried to go with them, but they could not start off that fast. They established their position during the first mile and fell into a comfortable pace. Devon would not stay at this pace for long. He was not settling for less and not answering to anyone in this race. While making a sharp right turn at the mile, another runner tried to cut him off on the inside. Devon gave him a sharp elbow to the chest and the other runner went down. He was not letting anyone test him today. He was on a war path, and no one could stop him.

At the front of the race, Dave kept up with the leaders as they distanced themselves from the rest of the competitors. Dave was determined to finish in the top three. He had raced against two of the favorites to win this race many times and was going to stick to them like glue the entire race. They flew through the second mile. Dave had never run so fast in a race before, and this was supposed to be a slow course. Approaching the two-mile marker, Dave glanced at the time. The clock read 10:03. This was by far the fastest start to a race he ever had, and there was still more than a mile to go. He didn't care. As the last runner fell off the pace, Dave looked at who he was running with. It was exactly who he wanted it to be. The two runners he had his eye on before the race. Dave put his head down and headed into the last mile.

As the runners that had gone out in front dropped back, Devon would pass them up. He just kept speeding up. He didn't know how fast he was running; he didn't know what place he was in; all that he knew was the furious desire that relentlessly drove him today. His rage could only be lessened by passing another runner, and that is what he did. Throughout the second mile, he must have moved up ten places. He came out of a series of sharp turns and approached a long two hundred meter straightaway that ended with the marker signaling the start of the last mile. Devon stretched out his long legs and powered through this straightaway. He shook off two runners that had been trying to keep up with him and passed up another that had fallen back from the front. His two-mile time was roughly 10:15; only a second off his best time ever for two miles. It still wasn't fast enough. There was only one runner left that was able to stick with him. He was just one more person Devon couldn't wait to discard.

The last mile wound through the forest preserve and spit the lead runners out near where they had started the race. There was a quarter-mile to go. Dave had run quarter-miles before. He had run twenty-five of them every Monday in the blazing summer heat for more than two months. A quarter-mile was nothing compared to the thousands of miles he had run in his life. One of the runners had separated from the group and would not be caught. It was down to Dave and the other contestant. They approached two hundred meters to go, running neck-and-neck. Dave dug down deep for everything he had. They flew through the finish line. Dave had barely been beaten out, but it didn't matter. He had just taken third place in one of the most competitive meets in the state and almost beaten two runners who were locks to be All-State this year. Moments after he finished, he looked back to see someone fly through the finish whom he did not expect to see. He hadn't seen this person finish so closely to him all year. It warmed Dave's heart to see who it was.

Winding through the last mile of the race, Devon and his opponent jockeyed for position, but there was only one scenario that Devon would accept. He had worked too long and too hard to just give in to fatigue. He was tired, and his legs screamed with pain. Nevertheless, he kept speeding up. One step at a time, he pulled ahead of his would-be challenger. Emerging from the trees, the first thing Devon saw was Coach Keogh. His coach was adamant: "Devon! Three hundred meters to go; give it everything you have right now!" It looked as though he might have a heart attack if he were anymore excited. That was all Devon needed to hear. He disposed of his competitor and sprinted through the final quarter-mile with reckless abandon. The last two hundred meters were a straightaway lined with screaming spectators. The noise, the insanity, pushed him even harder. He crossed the line just five seconds behind Dave. The look of intensity on his face quickly turned into one of relief. He had finally emerged as one of the top runners in the state. He finally had a race that he could say he truly dominated. He and Dave congratulated each other and looked back. It only got better from here.

Steve had been constantly passing people during the entire race as well. He dispatched many of the runners that Dave and Devon had sent back his way. He was finally in great shape and knew it. Using his great natural speed, he continuously surged past competitors throughout the race. Going through the final mile, he had one runner left to beat. The two went into the woods together, and Steve reemerged running all alone. With a strong finish, he crossed line in eleventh place with his best performance all year. It kept getting better for the Mustangs.

Craig built on his own momentum during this race. He cruised past one racer after another. Battling through his own injuries and silencing any doubt his teammates may have had about him, he finished with another great time. Andrew left Andy behind with a mile to go and finished twelve seconds behind Craig. Andy wasn't far behind him, and Sunil came in five seconds behind Andy.

At the awards ceremony after the race, only the top four runners were given medals and deservedly so. Downers South's two horses proudly accepted their awards and rejoined their team. Many runners looking over the results after the race were puzzled. "This can't be right," many of them exclaimed, "Downers South doesn't have runners that are that fast." The Mustangs' two studs were finally running together again. The team finished a strong second place and joyously celebrated as they headed home. The Conference Championship was in one week, and they felt ready for it. This race had been a terrific springboard heading into the month-long State Series. That night they all celebrated together and enthusiastically speculated on the coming weeks. They couldn't bask in their glory for too long though. There was still much work to be done.

Four Points

The team met for practice on Monday, excited to start the State Series and excited to start their new workout regimen. They designed a rigorous workout routine for the last month of the season which was supposed to have them running their best for the biggest races of the year. Conference would be the first challenge waiting for them. The team had been looking forward to this race ever since their embarrassing loss to Hinsdale South a month earlier. They wanted payback. They were a different team now and felt confident they could come back and beat Hinsdale to finish in a first place tie in the Conference.

The nine members competing for the varsity team stepped onto the track for their first workout of the new regimen. It was a two-mile time trial in spikes followed by two individual miles in heavier training shoes. This was designed to build up their speed and strength. Each week, the workout would get progressively easier in order for the team to be a little more rested as the meets became more difficult. Dave, Devon, and Steve led the way followed by the rest of the group competing for the last four spots on varsity. Many people were anxious to see how this team would do. They often talked of how excited they were to redeem their performance at Sectionals from a year ago, and now it was time to see if they could back it up. Several parents and other family members of the runners and coaches assembled outside of the track to see this team begin its final march towards glory. Many were excited to see how Devon and Dave would finish the season. They had been fixtures on the varsity team for three years now, and everyone wanted them to finish their high school cross country careers on top.

The workout was grueling for everyone. They were all tired from the race they had just run two days ago. After watching their team's workout, Coaches Keogh and Bicicchi agreed to bring Chris back up to varsity for the first time since he had gotten hurt. He would be replacing Sunil. Sunil had put forth a great effort over the season and had been invaluable to the team's success, but his lack of training before the season finally caught up with him. He was just too worn out to keep putting forth the fantastic performances he had consistently shown all season. The team running for redemption at Conference would be Dave, Devon,

Steve, Andy, Craig, Chris, and Andrew. They were all anxious and ready to go out give Hinsdale all they could handle.

As the runners assembled to board the bus on Saturday morning, their resolve was strong, but they were not all too thrilled about the weather today. It was windier than it had been when they faced Hinsdale on the very same course a month ago, and the temperature was much lower. It had even snowed the day before. The temperature when they arrived at the course was a chilly forty-five degrees with wind gusts up to forty miles per hour. These were less than ideal conditions to have their best performance of the year. Nevertheless, they all remained focused on the task at hand.

As the last race of the day approached, the varsity team stripped off most of the layers they had piled on to stay warm and began their warm-up jog. Dave, Devon, and Steve knew it was up to them to get up in front and split up Hinsdale's top two runners. The Mustangs' strength was their top three horses, and the team's chances of success rested largely on them. The seven teammates huddled up and listened to Coach Keogh give an impassioned speech. They had never seen him so adamant and intense before a race. He wanted this win just as bad as they did. The team stepped to the line, ignoring the wind whipping across them, and listened to the starter.

Bang!

At the sound of the gun they were off to reclaim their Conference Title. Immediately, Dave and Devon took the lead. They both wanted to establish themselves at the front of the race early on. There was no mistaking who would be competing for the Conference Championship at the start of the race. All but three of the top fifteen runners were either from Hinsdale or Downers South. At the front of the race, Hinsdale's top two runners and the Mustangs' top two runners ran together. Dave was determined to win. He was unbeaten in the Conference so far this season and had every intention of ending it that way. At the mile, Hinsdale's Lee Vlcek took the lead with Dave following him closely. Devon and Brian Denk battled each other not far behind.

About ten seconds behind Devon was Steve. He had separated by a considerable margin from the rest of the race and was stuck by himself getting slammed by the wind on the wide open course. Despite this, Steve had his sights fixed on Devon and was determined to close the gap between them. After Steve, there was a considerable gap until the next group of runners could be seen. Andy was among this group. He was running his best race since the Mustang Invite. He ran up with three runners from Hinsdale and another runner from Morton. About fifteen seconds behind this group were Chris, Craig, and Andrew. They were working off each other but not having their strongest performances of the season. They still felt the effects of that workout from Monday and fought to keep up with the rest of the race. Regardless, Downers South's top four runners were in great position and looked like they might be able to make this race a victory for the Mustangs.

During the second mile, everything went wrong. Dave was having his worst race of the season. Lee Vlcek pulled ahead of him and put considerable ground between the two of them. Not long after that, Brian Denk passed him by as well. He left Devon behind shortly after the mile and quickly moved his way up, trying to catch up with his teammate. The Mustangs would not be able to win if Hinsdale took the top two spots in the race. Dave and Devon knew this but were powerless to do anything about it. They felt as if they didn't have their legs under them. They would grit their teeth and try to close some ground, but no matter how hard they tried, they just kept getting pushed back by the wind. Going into the last mile, the race was over. Dave, Devon, and Steve finished in third, fourth, and fifth place. Andy ran a gutsy race and managed to just barely beat Hinsdale's fourth runner and almost beat their third as well. He ended up in seventh place. Chris, Craig, and Andrew finished alongside each other in thirteenth, fourteenth, and fifteenth place. The Mustangs had come close but lost by just four points.

During the awards presentation, not one of the Mustangs' runners dared to crack a smile. As they watched their rivals celebrate and hoist their Conference Championship trophy above their heads, no one took it harder than Dave and Devon. Dave had not finished below first place in a Conference race all year. In the meet against Hinsdale earlier that season, Dave had finished well ahead of Hinsdale's top two runners. Now, he had to taste the sour flavor of defeat after a lackluster performance. Devon, once again, watched another one of his dreams slip away. He had finished in the exact same place last year at Conference, easily beating the three runners that beat him today. He had worked himself to exhaustion for almost a year to come back and have a legitimate shot at winning. He wanted to build off of his success from last week to come out and make a statement to start the State Series today. Instead, he was going home with his tail tucked between his legs. As the team made its way back to the bus, Devon's frustration boiled over. He reached into his backpack, took his fourth place medal out, and threw it in the trash. This was just another disappointment in a very disappointing season for him. Coach Keogh was upset but carried a confidence about him. He reassured his team that next week at the Regional Meet when they face Hinsdale again, things would be different. His runners took his word for it and put this behind them. They had more important things to worry about than the Conference Title. They were still focused on avenging their loss at Sectionals last year and going down to State.

Yield to Nothing

The team headed into the same Regional as they had last year. They would be facing the same teams on the same course. Many of the same runners were returning, which meant it would be that much more competitive than it had been the year before. The coaches were making it very clear to their team that this would be a battle. They would only advance if they put forth a great performance. Devon knew this very well. He was getting so close to his chance to redeem his poor performance in last year's Sectional, he could taste it. One thing that he and Dave had focused on from the very start was making sure the team was ready when it counted. When Devon woke up Sunday morning after Conference, he wrote out a speech that he would give to his teammates when they huddled up before the race on Saturday. Just thinking of delivering the speech got his heart racing. He couldn't wait to get out there with a follow-up of last year's dominating performance he had put on at Regionals.

First thing was first for the Mustangs. They had their time trial workout on Monday. This time, they would run a three-mile race in spikes and finish up with a mile in training shoes. They stepped out onto the track on a cold and rainy afternoon. The conditions were less than ideal for running, but they were on a mission and nothing was going to stand in their way. As they began the workout, their three horses, Dave, Devon, and Steve, took a huge lead on their teammates. They were almost thirty seconds in front of the next runner at the mile. The three of them would run through the adverse conditions to finish close to 15:05 for three miles. This was just a practice that they were running two days after an exhausting race, and it looked as if they were not even tired. The coaches could not wait to see the kind of damage their three front-runners could do against this competitive field on Saturday. After the top three finished, things did not look as promising. The rest of the team did look as if they had just run a race two days before and came in more than a minute behind Dave, Devon, and Steve. One of the first runners in this group was Matt. He had been hamstrung by his torn ligament all year, but today, he ran with a purpose that impressed his coaches and teammates. Matt had a shot of making varsity with a strong performance at Conference, but he tragically had to come late to the race from his grandfather's funeral. His race was over before he even began. His heart was heavy, and the last thing on his mind was a race. He ran courageously but did not come close to cracking back into the top seven. Today was a different story. He ran like he had something to prove and got his point across. He was fit and ready to make it onto varsity if any of them should perform poorly at Regionals.

Friday night, the team met at Steve's house for their team dinner. They had a surprise waiting for them for the second year in a row. Unbeknownst to them, Coach Bicicchi and Coach Keogh went out and bought them all new uniforms for the State Series again. These were even better than last year's. The top was white with dark blue shorts. "DGS" was written diagonally in cursive lettering across the front with the team's mascot of a mustang in mid-stride displayed prominently on the back. The idea again was for them to be able to easily spot each other from any point on the course, and these new uniforms made that very possible. They looked great and were made of the highest quality light-weight fiber. They fit each individual perfectly. Now this team was ready for battle. They looked like warriors, and indeed, they needed to feel as if they were heading into battle. The task that lay in waiting for them tomorrow would be a monumental challenge.

The team boarded the bus the next morning. For the second year, this was the best Regional in the state by a long shot. For the second year, this was the best Regional in state history. The Mustangs headed back into the breach. The runners stepped off the bus and set up camp. Many of them were very nervous. Few had slept well last night. Last year's squad had been a veteran team that had run in these kinds of races before. From this team, only Dave and Devon had ever run in a race of this magnitude before. The weather today was almost identical to what it had been last year; overcast and cool. The weather was ideal, but the course was in awful shape. It rained heavily all week. The entire course was a slop of mud. There would be no course records set today. Only the strongest runners would survive in conditions such as these.

As the team warmed up, they passed by Hinsdale South. They looked with scorn at the team they had come so close to beating out for the Conference Title only a week ago. Dave, Devon, and Steve had let the team down last week, but they vowed to not have a repeat performance today. Coach Keogh carried the quiet confidence he had exhibited after last week's disappointing loss. He knew that Hinsdale had won last week because there were no other runners to break up their team. They and the Mustangs were head and shoulders ahead of the rest of the competition at Conference. Today was a different story. With so many good runners, many spots would be filled in between the large gap between Hinsdale's second and third runners. This would work to the Mustangs advantage. He couldn't wait to see how this race would play out.

The varsity made their way over to the starting line. They huddled around the coaches for their speech. Coach Bicicchi made his point loud and clear; "Last year we were here, this year we're back! Let none of these other teams forget who we are and what we're made of."

They all got the point. They broke it out and the coaches left their team at the start. After doing some practice starts, they had their runners-only huddle. After Dave said a few words of encouragement, their focus shifted to Devon. He had been waiting for this all week; "We are up against the best the state has to throw at us today. The course is tough and the competition is tougher, but we must not let anything stand in between us and our dreams. You will yield to nothing! And I know you won't." If they hadn't been energized enough after hearing from Coach Bicicchi, Devon certainly hammered the point home. The seven of them headed back to the starting line and listened as the starter called out the final commands.

As the starter spoke to the racers waiting to get going, the seven of them thought to themselves. Devon and Dave thought back about last year's team. This race had been their defining moment last year, where the team turned the heads of the entire state. Today was their chance to come back as seniors and lead their young team to glory. Steve calmly listened to the starter's instructions echoing across the starting line. He had a great week of practice and had been improving with every race this season. Today, he too would emerge as another contender for All-State on this team. He was ready, and he knew it. Andy was determined to put forth another strong performance. Last week he had run well but fell just short of scoring the points his team needed to win. He wouldn't make that same mistake again. Chris and Andrew had never been so nervous. Looking at all these runners they were lined up next to, the two of them took in the immensity of this venue. They felt like they were in over their heads. They feared that they weren't ready. Craig was ready to make everyone forget about last week's performance. He made no difference in the scoring whatsoever at Conference, and he was not going to let that happen on this grand stage. The seven of them snapped back to reality when they heard the starter say, "on your marks…get set."

Bang!

Immediately, there was trouble. The starting line was very muddy, and Devon slipped on his first step and almost fell over. After spending the first fifty meters trying to regain his balance, he looked ahead to see the rest of the race had sprinted out in front of him. He went into a dead sprint to catch up. The adrenaline from almost falling pushed him a little too hard. He ran all the way to the front of the race. This wouldn't last for long. He started out way too fast, and he knew it. Along with getting off to a rough start his legs felt sluggish. He had not tapered back his training enough and felt the effects of that now. It would be a very long three miles.

The rest of the team got off to a fine start and quickly fell into a comfortable pace. Some were more comfortable than others. Dave was off to his typical fast start towards the front of the race. He knew it was imperative that he place highly in the race to get the team off to a good start. After a mile, he was doing just that. He established himself in the top five and looked as if he was not going to slow up. A few spots back, Devon had fallen back from his fast start and kept pace with Steve. Steve pushed the pace faster than Devon could handle though. After they passed the mile marker, Steve surged ahead and Devon would spend the rest of the race trying to catch up with him. After Devon, there was a very long gap until another Downers South jersey could be seen. Andy ran about forty seconds behind Devon. Craig, Chris, and Andrew were a little further behind him. The Mustangs' top three were performing great once again, but it was up to their other four runners to see if they would make it to Sectionals.

Dave had returned to form for the right race. Last week's disappointing performance seemed like it had been weeks ago. Going into the last mile, he had fallen out of the top five but was running with two others runners, including one of Hinsdale's top runners, Lee Vlcek, battling for sixth place. He knew he was stronger than both of them and was just waiting for his opportunity to make a move. With a half-mile to go, he went ahead of them and didn't look back. His hard work over the last several months had paid off. He outlasted them throughout the middle of the race and still had enough energy to put them away at the end. He crossed the line in sixth place and looking very strong doing so. Dave had been the Mustangs' top finisher in every race this season and held true to form once again.

This was Steve's breakout race. He had never run even close to this well all season. He spent the entire race trying to catch up to Dave, but Dave just ran too well. Nevertheless, Steve was in great position going into the last half-mile. He was competing with three other runners for a spot in the top ten. They kept trying to speed up and leave him behind but were unsuccessful in doing so. He stuck right with them and coming into the final quarter-mile, he was right where he wanted to be. Putting on a speed burst, he left some other runners trying to catch up behind him and was fighting for tenth place. Climbing the final hill that led to the finish line, it was between him and two other competitors to see who would finish in tenth place. He just barely got edged out coming across the line and had to settle for eleventh. Eleventh place was fine with him and the rest of his team. He just had his best performance of the season during the biggest race of the season. He did everything he needed to do and more for his team.

Devon was in pain the entire race. He practiced too hard during the week and was paying for it now. He fought with everything he had just to maintain his position. Heading into the last mile, he felt as if he would barely be able to finish. Despite this, he continued to fight on. He was even able to catch up to Steve, who had been well ahead of him the entire race, with a half-mile to go. He stuck with the pack competing for the top ten but when it came down to the last quarter-mile, he was toast. Devon gritted his teeth and put his head down to give everything he had on this last stretch, but there wasn't much left to draw upon. He forced one leg in front of the other. His legs felt as if they weighed one hundred pounds each. Fighting with every muscle in his body, he crossed the line in thirteenth place. Devon had not done as well as the coaches had hoped, but Steve's amazing performance made up for that. After he crossed the line, him, Dave, Steve, and coaches looked back and waited. They would be waiting for much too long.

Finally, they saw Andy emerge at the bottom of the hill that began the final hundred meters. This was a good fifty seconds after Devon had finished. That was too much time in a race this competitive. In those fifty seconds, twenty-seven places passed between Devon and Andy. It would be up to the fifth runner to keep this team alive.

Craig had started out further back in the race with Chris and Andrew but about half-way through the race, began to speed up. He kept gaining ground, building momentum, and kept passing other runners up. With a half-mile to go, this was his chance to make his mark on this team. He had run well all year but had not come up clutch in any of the big races. Today would be different. Craig kept digging hard and putting other runners behind him. He saw Andy a few places ahead of him and was quickly catching up. He would not catch up to Andy, but he would finish with his biggest performance of the year. Twenty seconds after Craig finished, Chris and Andrew crossed the line. The coaches were not sure what to make of their team's performance. They had run well, but it would be very close between them and two other teams to see who would advance. It was very possible that the Mustangs may not make it through this race.

After the race, the Downers Grove South camp was quiet. They all tensely awaited the results to be tallied up and printed. When they finally arrived, the team breathed a collective sigh of relief. Hinsdale South had better enjoy that Conference trophy, because their team's season was over. The Mustangs finished in fourth place, and Hinsdale had finished in sixth. Downers South beat them by a mere six points. It was their turn to break their rival's hearts. Hinsdale's top two runners would advance as individuals, but the rest of their team would be going home for the winter. The Mustangs had won on the strength of their top three horses once again and on a gutsy performance by their stand-out sophomore.

After the bus arrived back at school, the coaches told their team to go home and rest up. They barely survived a close one, and next week would be a completely different story. Coach Keogh and Coach Bicicchi talked long after their runners had left. Their team had run well but not that well. They needed to send a message. This team was going to be successful no matter what sacrifices needed to be made. The time trial on Monday would not just be a workout; it was going to be a try-out to see who would run at Sectionals. They had learned their lesson from last year. Their team did not need to be relaxed going into next weekend. They needed to be ready for the greatest challenge of their lives.

How Long Must You Wait for It?

This Sectional race was something the likes of which the state had never seen before. All of the same teams from the year before would be returning with most of the same runners. These teams which had been so great a year ago brought back a majority of the same athletes and were now that much better. Those that qualified through this Sectional would all have a legitimate shot to finish in the top ten in the state. This ultra competitive race would be run on one of the toughest courses one could find in the state. The race moved to a different location this year. The course was five kilometers, which was longer than the usual distance of three miles. This added at least another minute onto the hardest race of the year. This course was also one of the toughest because it was one long steep hill after another. There was a hill two miles into the race that had an incline of at least forty-five degrees. It resembled a wall more than a hill. On top of all this, it continued to rain throughout the week before the race. To get to the State Meet, the Mustangs would have to run through 3.1 miles of mud and hills, and against the best competition the state had to offer.

The coaches knew what their team was up against so they tapered back the training schedule for the week. Their only hard workout would be a mile and a half time trial on Monday to determine who would be running at Sectionals. The varsity met out on the track and got started on this race. Dave won it with Steve not far behind him. Devon did not look good. He trailed behind Dave and Steve the entire race and did not look like he had much energy. The weight of a year of expectations bore down on him. After his somewhat disappointing performance at Regionals, he worried that he would not be good enough to avenge his performance from last year. He was afraid that all of his hard work and dedication would be for nothing in the end, and he would end the season having done so much for no real reward. All of this ran through Devon's mind as he ran this time trial.

Behind the top three, it was a battle for the last four spots. Andy and Craig led the way, with Chris, Andrew, and Matt following closely. If anyone was going to break into the top seven, it would be Matt. He had been practicing great the last two weeks after his grandfather passed away. After Chris and Andrew's poor performances at Regionals, the coaches decided that the team needed to understand that nothing less than excellence would be tolerated. If someone was not feeling like they could achieve that, then they would be replaced by someone that could. Coming into the last lap, it was between Chris, Andrew, and Matt for the final two spots. Chris pulled ahead coming around the final turn. Matt moved in front of Andrew, and he could see the finish. All that he had to do was beat him for the last hundred meters, and he would be on varsity for the first time in two months. Andrew was not going down so easily though. He had worked tirelessly all season. He ran varsity every race, and nothing was going to stop him from running in the biggest race of the year. Pushing off of his toes, he sprinted ahead and barely beat out Matt crossing the line. The same team would be running at Sectionals, but the message had been made loud and clear: Saturday would require an exceptional performance from every one of them and if anyone was not feeling up to the challenge, they had better get out of the way.

The seven of them left team dinner on Friday night early to get their rest. Tomorrow was going to be the biggest challenge of their lives. None of them had ever faced a task so daunting. Together they would stand, or together they would fall. Each of them went home thinking over what lay ahead the next morning. They had worked so hard for so long. Would it pay off? Would all those miles, all those speeches they heard, and all of the adversity they had overcome be worth it in the end? It all came down in the end to one thing: would they make it to the Promised Land?

Devon opened his eyes. He looked around his room. It was still dark. He looked at the clock on his cell phone. It was four o'clock in the morning. He thought about trying to go back to sleep but knew it would do no good. He was wide awake. He had been waiting an entire year for this day. There was no way he could sleep for such a momentous occasion. He had been feeling a lot of fear and uncertainty early on in the week, but it all subsided when he remembered something Mr. Newton had told him: "The secret of success in life is for a man to be ready when his opportunity comes." Devon was ready. He had been waiting for three hundred and sixty-five days for this opportunity. He lay awake in bed for a long time envisioning the race. He envisioned the pain he would experience, the mental and physical barriers he would have to overcome, and knew that this was going to be the race of his life. For a whole year he had been carrying the weight of the world on his shoulders, and today was his chance to throw it off. It didn't matter what happened in the end after he finished this race. It didn't matter if he made it to State or not. All that mattered was that he went out there and left it all out on that course. He did not want to look back after it was all over and know in his heart that he could have done more. He knew that feeling all too well. That is what had happened last year at Sectionals, and there was no way in hell that would happen today.

The team met at school to take the bus over to the course. Many of them had solemn looks on their faces. They knew they were headed into the snake pit and were not sure what was going to happen once it was all said and done. All of them had that same look on their face except for Devon. He walked up with a smile from ear to ear. He saw Coach Bicicchi and Joe and went up to them boasting about how he had been awake for five hours already. Both of them knew he was ready for this. The question was; were his teammates as prepared?

The team boarded the bus; each runner alone in a seat, turned their iPods on, and thought about what might happen in the coming hours. Dave was also getting himself prepared for the race of his life. He knew just as well as Devon what kind of effort this would require. He knew the pressure was on him to be the number one runner and get out in front for his team. He prepared himself mentally for the enormous task that lay ahead of him. Perhaps he was thinking just a little too much because he felt nervous for the first time all year. There were all sorts of "what if" questions circling through his head. He worried what would happen if he did not run as well as he needed to. The pressure was building.

There was a song that made Devon think of last year's Sectional every time he heard it. He had purposely refrained from listening to it all season because he was waiting until today to draw on those feelings. He clicked play on his iPod and listened to the opening chords for the first time in months. As the song played on, he reflected on what had happened one year ago today. He thought about the fear and uncertainty that had gripped him before the race had started. He thought about the crushing feeling of unavoidable defeat that he had felt at the starting line. He thought about how he had let his teammates down with his poor performance. He thought about those five seniors that never had gotten a chance to go to State with a team because he let his fear get the best of him. He pictured himself crying like a baby after watching those other teams celebrate after they qualified for State. This all stoked a raging inferno inside of him. Today was going to be different. As another song came on that he often listened to for motivation, he sat up in his seat and looked out the front of the bus. He sat up to face the challenge that lay ahead. He sat up to face his destiny.

The bus arrived at the Sectional course. The team got out, set up camp, and relaxed before they started their warm-ups. After they all had time to take it easy, Dave and Devon gathered their teammates. The time had come. They started their warm-up jog and took their first steps toward the race of their lives.

The seven of them returned to camp from their warm-up jog and readied themselves for the race. They stretched, laced up their spikes, shed a few layers of clothing they had bundled themselves up with, and headed over to the line. The coaches spoke with them but did not have much to say. Everyone knew what this was and everyone knew what was expected. The coaches left their team at the line, and now it was just the seven of them. After running a few sprints, the seven of them huddled up, perhaps for the last time, to listen to their captains. Devon immediately spoke; "I won't lie to you guys, the odds are definitely stacked against us. Not too many people are expecting much out of us today. There are a lot of good runners here." His teammates were confused about his negative message. This was supposed to motivate them? Devon continued on; "Well you want to know something about everyone else here?

SCREW 'EM! We're good and we're going to State. If anyone doesn't think so get the hell out of here right now. We have come so far and worked so hard. Today we'll show everyone just how ready we are. We're going to go out there and give 'em hell today. Give 'em hell on three; one, two, three, GIVE 'EM HELL".

They were ready. Seven men, seven warriors headed back to the line. They looked to their left and to their right. They looked at the hundreds of other runners that were here today. Screw 'em. They had not come this far to let these other guys steal their hopes and dreams away from them.

They anxiously stood at the starting line and listened to the starter give his commands. A cold wind whipped across their faces. It all came down to this. Devon had pictured this exact moment since he had seen the course for the first time a month earlier when the team had come here to run a practice. He had pictured looking at the initial straight-away, the biting cold wind blowing across his body, the voice of the starter talking through his megaphone, the collective tenseness of two hundred runners standing on the doorstep of glory; he was ready for this.

Bang!

The starter fired his gun, and the race was off. Immediately, the entire race was stuck in gridlock. The entire first mile was filled with mud up to their ankles. This did not faze the Mustangs. They had trained for conditions such as this. They had built up their strength and toughness for six months to plow through adverse conditions such as these. Dave, Devon, and Steve ran together for the first half-mile. They tucked in behind three runners and let them bear the brunt of the wind. Slopping their way through the mud, they persevered on. It might as well have been a track for all they cared. They were so focused on their goal that nothing was going to discourage them.

Dave then moved ahead and was moving very quickly. He knew he needed to get a high place, but he let his emotions override his better judgment and sprinted up with the leaders of the race. Dave was used to running with the leaders of races, but he had not seen runners of this quality all year. Pacing with the top runners in this race meant that one was a top ten runner in the state. Dave was accustomed to starting out fast, but going out too fast on a course like this could spell disaster. After nearly getting their shoes sucked off in the mud, the runners ran past the mile marker into the portion of the race that wound through a forest preserve. This leg of the race pitted the contestants through two miles of steep hills. After the first hill, Dave began to fall back. He knew he was going too fast and needed to slow his pace if he was to run a strong race. He rounded a bend and headed down a very long and steep hill. After going down this hill, the course made a one hundred and eighty degree turn and went right back up the same hill. It was at this point, that Dave felt the toll that going out so hard had taken on him. Scaling this incline that seemed to have no end slowly but surely broke him down. Half-way up, he saw someone speed past him and effortlessly power his way up the rest of the hill. It was Devon.

Devon had never felt so at home in a race. He loved facing adversity. He was at his best when the odds were overwhelmingly stacked against him. The first mile of thick mud made no difference to him. He would run three miles through quicksand if that was what it would take today. He had felt particularly encouraged about this race after seeing the course for himself earlier in the season. Devon thrived on courses that favored strong runners. There were runners who were faster than him, but few could say they were stronger. Hills were the parts of races where Devon had a clear advantage over his competition. Coming into the part of the race that consisted of two miles of steep hills was just where Devon wanted to make his move. He flew down the long downhill and turned around to scale the steep uphill. He put his head down, pushed off of his toes, and left at least ten runners behind him by the time he emerged at the top. He continued onward through the second mile. Up and down these steep hills, he pressed on. At the two-mile marker was the hill that was referred to as the wall. One had to hurdle themselves up a very sharp incline and then climb another two hundred meters running uphill. Devon bounded up the wall and painstakingly ran up the rest of the hill. By the time he got to the top, he was so exhausted he could barely catch his breath. His legs were screaming at him. For the first time in the entire race, he doubted if he could continue on.

Joe waited at this point because he knew this would be where the team needed encouragement. Going into the last mile of the biggest race of their lives, and after having been pushed to the brink by the toughest course in the state, their determination would be hanging by a thread. As he saw Devon emerge at the crest of the hill, he knew that his friend needed help. The look on his face was one of complete and utter exhaustion. He ran up and screamed words of encouragement in Devon's face. If Joe had gotten any closer to him, he would have been in the race himself. Joe pointed out the top runner from another team that was directly in front of him. He told Devon to catch up to him and not leave his side. Joe thought of anything and everything he could to keep his friend going and give him courage to finish out the rest of the race.

After hearing Joe's encouraging words, something came into Devon's head. He pictured himself crying a year ago today. He thought to himself; "What is more painful, this race or the shame of defeat?" That was all he needed to hear. He put his doubt and fatigue in the back of his head and continued on. One step after another, he closed in on the runner in front of him. There was one final hill he had to climb. He sped to the top and now ran alongside two other competitors. They turned the corner to head into the final quarter-mile of the race. Devon could see the finish. As he prepared to give everything he had in this final stretch, something held him back. It was the mud. They were going to run this final and crucial part of the race in deep and sloppy mud. No one could move in this quagmire. The position a runner was in going into this mud, was the position they would stay in. The three runners emerged out of the mud field and had solid ground to run on for the final hundred meters of the race. It all came down to this. A year of expectations, pain, and dedication all came down to one hundred meters.

Devon came out of the mud sprinting. He was exhausted, cold, and wet, but that made no difference. With every last ounce of energy left in his body, he gave it everything he had. He could barely see in front of him because his brain was deprived of oxygen. All he knew was that he couldn't slow his torrid pace. He flailed his arms and forced each leg to go in front of the other. Finally, it was over. He crossed the line having beaten out one of the competitors he was running with and having only been beaten out by a step by the other one. This was the hardest and most exhausting race he had ever run in his life, and he had dominated it. He looked back to see if his teammates had fared just as well.

As Devon passed Dave by, going up that long and steep hill about half-way through the race, Dave knew he was in trouble. Going out too fast on a course such as this could prove disastrous. By the time Dave climbed to the top of this hill, Devon was far ahead of him and Steve passed him up as well. Dave had been going backwards in this race since he crossed the first mile marker. As he trudged through the hills that consisted of the next mile of the race, he just felt more and more beat down. Coming into the race he had so much pride and confidence in himself after an incredible season, but all of that didn't mean anything now. He felt as if he had nothing left by the time he crossed the two-mile marker, and he still had more than a mile to go. As he ran the last quarter-mile through the mud, he felt as if he was on a death march. He crossed the line thirty seconds behind Devon and twenty seconds behind Steve. His season was over. After coming so far, it all came to a tragic end on this cold miserable day in late October. Dave was devastated. After being so dominant all season, this is how his senior season would end. He quickly walked back to the camp. He was so embarrassed and ashamed he could not even look at anyone.

As Steve passed Dave going up the hill, he knew he was going to have another good race. He felt strong, and his legs felt quick. Going through the up and down hills in the middle of the race, he once again was passing runners at will. He was determined to catch up with Devon. If Dave wasn't going to have a good race, then it would be up to Devon and him to pick up the slack. As Steve climbed the wall just past the second mile marker, his momentum that he had been building came to a halt. It felt as if this last daunting hill might be the one that could break him. As he neared the top he was completely exhausted and had no idea how he was going to run another mile. He was not this tired at the end of most races, much less in the middle of them. Joe saw Steve emerge at the top of the hill and did everything he could to get him going too. After Joe's words of inspiration, Steve was back on track. Joe had willed on the Mustangs' top two runners. He might not be able to run in this race, but he was doing everything he could to help his team.

Steve passed by Joe and got his wits about him once again. He returned his focus to the task at hand. He wasn't sure how the rest of his teammates were doing, but he knew he was going to do everything in his power to help this team make it to State. Steve was close to runners from the two teams they needed to beat. Coming into the last half-mile, he moved ahead of them and going into the mud, he was still in front. After fighting his way through the mud, he came out and finished his race with a fantastic last hundred meters. Putting the other two runners behind him, he sped across the finish line with another excellent performance.

Further back in the race, Andy was having another great performance. He started out a little too quick but had thought better of it early enough that it did not hurt his race. Andy felt the strength in his legs that was a result of the hardest work he had ever done in his life. This strength propelled him through the mud and over hills. His toughness and focus helped him forget that a cold biting wind was blowing against him and that his body was exhausted. Coming into the last quarter-mile, he was digging hard to catch a group of runners directly in front of him, but once they all got stuck in the mud, no one was moving anywhere. He managed to run a strong last hundred meters but couldn't catch the runners that were in front of him. Nevertheless, he still had another great performance when his team needed him.

Andrew and Chris were working together to make it through this race. They needed to. Everything their coaches and their captains had been telling them was right. This was the hardest race they had ever run. They took turns taking the lead and quickening the pace. The two friends even gave each other words of encouragement to keep each other going. Andrew took the lead and pulled Chris along behind him as they neared the end of the race. They trudged through the mud and finished the race one second apart. They both ran much better races than they had a week before and showed they deserved to be here.

Craig felt completely overwhelmed by this race. The enormity of this race was too much to take in for the sophomore. He was fast and strong, but he was not nearly prepared enough for conditions as tough as these. The other six members of varsity had been training for this since June. Craig had worked hard, but during the summer, he did not expect to be in this kind of position. His team depended on him to have another big performance like he had the week before. This was just too much for him. This race was a major undertaking for experienced seniors, much less a sophomore running here for the first time. He came in well behind Andrew and Chris.

Once they had all finished, it looked as if they had just fought a battle. All seven of them had looks of complete exhaustion on their faces. They had mud all over them. Dave was off to the side being consoled by one of his friends. Everyone was trying to make sense out of what had just happened. How well had they done? Were they going to make it to State? The coaches knew the answer before all of them had crossed the line.

For the second year in a row, the Mustangs would not be making it to State, but for the second year in a row they would be sending one representative to run in Peoria. Devon had run the race of his life, and it paid off. He would be advancing as an individual qualifier. In what should have been a proud moment for Devon, he didn't know what to think. All along, he had dreamed of leading his team to glory at State and now, it would just be him. At the very least, he wanted to be down there running with Dave. The two friends had trained together all along and had never really thought that just one of them would be running in Peoria at the end of the season.

After Coach Keogh broke the news to Devon, he walked off with a bewildered look on his face. He sat alone on a picnic table not knowing what to make out of the situation. Coach Bicicchi sat next to him. Holding back tears Devon asked him; "What do I tell everyone? They have worked so hard and done everything we have asked of them, what do I tell them now?" His coach was just as broken up as he was but he pulled himself together, looked Devon in the eye and said; "Tell them how proud you are of everything they have done. You make it clear to them that they have so much to feel good about." Devon stayed where he was. He felt stunned. The rest of the team camp moved their way over to the awards ceremony, but Devon couldn't move. He stood up and looked around, as if there was something that he would see that would make everything alright. Joe saw his friend standing alone and went over to cheer him up. Devon almost burst into tears when he came over. He choked out; "I couldn't do it. I couldn't bring the team to State. Everything I've worked for is gone." Joe gave his good friend a hug and reassured him; "You're the greatest leader to ever come through this program and you just had the greatest race of your life in the most important race you've ever run in. You go over with your team and accept your State Qualifier award. You deserve it."

Devon gathered himself and went over to sit with his team. As they called him up to the stage to be recognized, it didn't feel right. He had pictured this moment as being a time when he and his teammates would be celebrating going down to State. He accepted his award and somberly made his way back to the bus.

The team boarded the bus to go back home. Their bodies and their hearts were weary from the long journey that had just abruptly ended. Dave was stretched so thin he couldn't even stay upset. He just felt this crushing feeling of defeat as he gazed out the window on the way back. This was not how Devon and Dave had envisioned their glorious campaign to avenge last year's loss would end.

On the ride home, Devon thought about his teammates. He didn't want them to just split apart the way last year's team had. He wanted them to have something to feel good about after this heartbreaking defeat. When the bus arrived back at school, he told the varsity team to meet in the locker room. Devon and Dave stood in front of their downtrodden teammates. Devon spoke first; "Dave and I just want to thank you all for everything you have done over the last few months. We did not expect much out of you before the summer started, and we can't even begin to describe how proud we are of how far you all have come. Don't let this bring you down. You all are great runners and will be a great team next year if you stick together." Dave let go of his grief for a moment and added; "This race was just ridiculous, and none of you should be ashamed of not making it through. We were up against some incredible odds, and you all did great. Don't ever think that none of the work you have put in is not worth it, because nothing could be farther from the truth."

A week later Devon ran at State. He got off to a good start, but a week after the biggest race of his life and without any teammates to run for, he finished with an average performance. It just wasn't the same without his brothers out there by his side. Regardless, he had finally done it. After a year of saving up all that guilt and shame from his poor performance at Sectionals as a junior, he came back and definitively threw the weight off of his shoulders. He endured through a trying summer of arduous training and a somewhat disappointing season, but in the end, he had accomplished his goal. His efforts finally paid off. He waited for a long time, but at last, had proved he could perform when his team needed him the most. He proved he could be a leader and be at his best when the pressure was the greatest. His performance at that Sectional had been more than great. It was more than gutsy and tough. It was legendary.

Land Amongst the Stars

As the team headed back from Sectionals that day, there was something that gave one a sense that change was abound. An eerie silence pervaded the usually raucous group as they wrapped up the long, exhausting campaign that they all had embarked upon together. For Dave and Devon, it had been a journey that had lasted close to three years, since they first dared to dream such lofty dreams as young up-and-coming sophomores. It was the kind of silence that follows any great event. For after every storm, a calm inevitably follows. For almost two years, there had been an undeniable energy about this team. They had been building strength and momentum for so long, but unfortunately, all great things must come to an end.

Indeed, many things would change after that cold, blustery, late autumn day in October of 2006. Things would never be the same as far as running went for the two captains. Both of them had successful track seasons and accepted offers to run at a Division I college together. After his senior track season, Dave would be plagued by injuries and sickness that eventually forced him to quit running. Devon ran on his college team for a year, but it just wasn't the same. He quit after a year to pursue other interests. For both Dave and Devon, that insatiable desire that had motivated them to work so tirelessly and drag their teammates along with them never fully returned. Such an immense undertaking is a very hard thing to repeat, and the fact that they were able to do it once was a miracle in itself. Coach Keogh and Coach Bicicchi always swore that they had never seen better leadership on any team they had been a part of, and both of them had run for State Qualifying teams in high school and National Qualifying teams in college.

In a controversial move, Coach Keogh would be let go by Downers Grove South to make room for a new teacher that wanted to be head coach. He accepted a job coaching with one of his old runners at a nearby school where he still coaches today. Coach Bicicchi would help out the new coach for another season. He stayed on to coach the rest of the team that he had coached the previous year. He now coaches with one of his good friends at another nearby school.

The rest of the team that returned for the next season had another successful year. Unfortunately, they were assigned to run in an even harder Sectional, with more great teams added in. No one would qualify individually from that team. Steve had a very good track season during his junior year, but it was cut short due to injuries which would hold him back as a senior. Andrew, Chris, Andy, Matt, and Craig would all have success in track as well. None of these runners would go onto run in college. Running on that great team at Downers South would be an experience too difficult to top.

Joe found his calling as a successful actor and director. He now helps his father coach, and has begun to run again. Devon and Dave would always be grateful to Joe for being their leader when everyone else depended on them. The three of them remain close friends to this day. Years later, many of the former teammates remain good friends. The coaches still keep in contact with some of their old runners as well. All of them will forever be linked by the amazing experience they all went through together.

Both of the teams were unique and special in their own way. The first team was a collection of egos that all thought they should be the best runner. The fact that those seven proud, stubborn individuals were able to put their differences aside and unite for one common dream was miraculous. This team takes the credit for establishing a tradition that still exists at Downers South today, even though everyone that was there when it began are now gone. They instilled the standard of greatness that carries through to each new team that wears a Downers Grove South uniform. That first team will always be remembered for making the Mustangs relevant in the state. Downers South was a team that no one ever thought twice about before the seven of them shocked everyone.

The next year's team was special for its outstanding leadership. The captains took a group of average runners and taught them to be great. A team that only returned two members to its varsity squad from the previous year came back to be just as dominant. Dave and Devon deserve the credit for making certain that the great team from the year before was not just a fluke. They ensured that Downers South would remain a team to be reckoned with and remain an outstanding program in the state for years to come. Even now, years after they have left, current runners still speak of those great teams of the past and strive to measure up to that standard.

During those two seasons, there may have been teams with more talent, but no other teams possessed the heart and desire of the Mustangs. Those two unbelievable years belonged to Downers Grove South. It was their time; not because of their success but because of what they symbolized. They were living evidence of the extraordinary things that are possible when a group of people commit themselves to a common goal. During that fleeting time, they elevated themselves above just being successful runners. They were something greater; something that one may only get to see once in a lifetime. They were the true embodiment of courage and hope; of loyalty and camaraderie; of joy and pain; of the elation of success and the heartbreak of defeat. They were legendary.

These two teams truly were a Cinderella story. Going from obscurity to greatness is something that is not often achieved, but this special group of individuals was able to make it happen. Those that had the chance to be a part of that great experience were lucky. Everyone that was involved still looks back and can draw motivation from that incredible ride they all shared. Those teams were living of proof of the old adage: "Shoot for the moon. Even if you miss, you will still land amongst the stars."

Epilogue

By: Coach Glenn Bicicchi

It is a privilege and honor to be called coach and with that comes the responsibility to motivate and to inspire. Running goes far beyond one's ability. It is the mindset that will make the difference for individual glory and for team success.

"The Bull Within" has been written by Mr. Kelly with a lot of heart and emotion. Its message is very clear; that you can be victorious by defeat. When you win, victory is so very sweet. That is why defeat is so much more bitter. However, it is only bitter if you swallow it. Two teams with different chemistries embraced their defeats only to make themselves better and to further their character, which in the end will be their destiny.

Cross Country is such a fabulous sport. As teammates you must have courage to be counted on. During a race there are so many variables that keep constantly changing: too fast, too slow, too hot, too cold, I was pushed, kicked, cut off and so on.

Team means whatever you are confronted with...together you will overcome.

You can't assume anything because the very moment you do, it is over. You cannot do a B+ performance and expect an A+ result. Whatever the task, it should be and will always require 110%. Only then will you meet and exceed expectations and greatness will then become your benchmark.

The heartbreak of not going to State has been a great lesson for all that were involved with this story. However, I believe that the runners will have learned true life lessons and will be doing amazing things; perhaps in athletics but in industry, medicine, journalism, teaching, and much more.

As teams we have won many medals and trophies, but in time, they will only tarnish and gather dust. It is their memories that will endure. They set the benchmark of excellence for future teams, and it is these teams that will look back on 2005 and 2006 with respect and admiration and realize that they entered their seasons as boys but left their mark as men.

Well done Mr. Kelly.

Respectfully,
Coach Glenn

About the author

Devon Kelly is a college student living in Bloomington, Illinois. He is the same Devon from the story. After graduating college he will be seeking employment as a social studies teacher. He has done extensive writing in pursuit of his degree which has developed his skills as a writer. About a year and a half ago he undertook this project to preserve the memory of this incredible experience for everyone involved. His future writing plans include writing a history of his mother and father's families.